Play
Better
Basketball

Play Better Basketball

An Illustrated Guide to Winning Techniques
and Strategies for Players and Coaches

Jim Pruitt

CONTEMPORARY
BOOKS, INC.
CHICAGO

Library of Congress Cataloging in Publication Data

Pruitt, Jim.
   Play better basketball.

   Includes index.
   Summary: A basketball coach discusses the
skills, techniques, attitudes, and characteristics
a coach looks for in a basketball player, at the
high school, college, amateur, or professional
level.
      1. Basketball—Juvenile literature.   2. Basket-
ball—Training—Juvenile literature.   3. Basketball—Vocational guidance—Juvenile literature.
[1. Basketball]   I. Title.
GV885.1.P78   1982   796.32'32   82-45427
ISBN 0-8092-5799-8

Published by Contemporary Books, Inc.
180 North Michigan Avenue, Chicago, Illinois 60601
Manufactured in the United States of America
Library of Congress Catalog Card Number: 82-45427
International Standard Book Number: 0-8092-5799-8

contents

foreword

Many basketball books have been written by coaches, presenting the different styles and systems with which they have had success, for the benefit of the young coach or the seasoned coach. In this book, *Play Better Basketball*, Jim Pruitt uniquely introduces his concepts and techniques to the athlete on the athlete's level. Particularly impressive is Jim's presentation of constructive, positive, motivating fundamentals for the athlete to follow. Here he answers many of the questions that young athletes ask in their goal of becoming good basketball players.

I highly recommend *Play Better Basketball* to young basketball players of all ages and also to coaches.

Gayle Hoover
Basketball Coach
with over 400 wins

preface

    This book is intended for my own players to use. It contains information I consider vital to any young basketball player who wishes to reach his or her full potential. My one regret is that I didn't write it sooner. I can't help but wonder how much better some of my top players might have been, or whether some average players might have become outstanding, had they had access to the information compiled here.

    This book began as a handbook for offseason preparation of ballplayers. Before its completion, I realized the handbook was more than that in its length and scope. It would serve a useful purpose as a book for young players who have dedicated themselves to being the best they can be. If that is your goal, this book is for you.

    Books written solely for the coach deal more with team offenses and defenses, game strategy, etc., and a player must wade through chapter after chapter to pick up anything he can apply on his own. *Play Better Basketball* gives directly to the athlete needed information on how to perform better in all areas of the game. The player can rely on his own ability and perseverance in applying the teaching in these pages, much of which might be overlooked by an inexperienced coach.

Jim Pruitt

chapter one

can you make the pros?

For almost everyone, the answer to the question posed above is, "Probably not." It would be unfair to delude young players into setting, and pinning their longings and expectations on, an unrealistic goal. *But don't be discouraged*. Read on! Let's take a very honest look at what it takes to become a professional basketball player and then examine some other options, which many find challenging, satisfying, and attainable.

The odds are roughly 10,000 to 1 that any high school player will become a pro someday. Staggering? Yes, to most. Insurmountable? Not to a sufficiently *talented, dedicated*, and *lucky* player.

As anyone who watches televised pro games can see, the ability displayed by pro players is phenomenal. Even a reserve on a professional team is a superb ball handler, shooter, passer, and defensive player. Players who get little or no playing time in pro games look bad only in comparison to the superstars who do play regularly. That doesn't mean the reserve is not a good player. Far from it! Put that reserve on a team with college players, even on a good college team, and he would probably look as superior to most of the other players as his professional teammates do to him.

More than half a million boys play basketball on high school teams in this country each year. Yet in the NBA there are only about 250 players, and only about 50 of them are rookies. If you divide 500,000 by 50, you get 10,000, which means that only one out of every 10,000 high school players will make the grade. The odds are a little better for girls, but only because fewer girls play basketball in high school. Girls get less encouragement from our changing, but still chauvinistic, society. Consequently, they must be strongly self-motivated to stick to the kind of training program required to reach the top. Even then, the rewards are fewer, particularly the financial ones.

Let's assume you are far better than the average player. You are a cat on defense and you've been netting 20 points a game. Your chances of turning pro are substantially better than 10,000 to 1, but they're still dismal: 350 to 1 might be an overly optimistic figure.

Now, let's say your team has an outstanding basketball tradition, including more than one trip to the state tournament, and is also having a very good season, being ranked in the top 20 in the state and winning almost all of its games. Your odds are getting better, because now your team may be noticed by scouts, who will look at it—and you. Of course, you could still try out for a college team without having been offered a scholarship, but in such a case the college will probably be a small, unheralded one, and again you could escape the notice of the next level of basketball scouts. But you're fortunate: they *have* taken a look at you. Now your odds, at best, could be 175 to 1. In other words, you can be good enough and lucky enough to win a scholarship to a large college and still have less than a 1% chance of making it to the pros!

We mustn't overlook the fact that most talented athletes may not be willing to pour as much sweat into their improvement efforts as you are. Just what sort of effort is required? A dedicated high school player must spend between two and 10 hours every day in practice. That's an *average*, not a once-in-a-while total. Without spending that much time on the sport, you have no hope at all of making your pro dreams come true. Are you truly ready to make a commitment that deep when, even with it, you may not reach your goal? Are you the sort of person who is so hopelessly in love with the game of basketball that even in freezing weather you put on a parka and gloves to go out and shoot baskets near the garage? Do you attend two or three clinics every summer? Are you still in the school gym an hour after practice, working on free throws, until the coach kicks you out so he can go home? Do you tell your girlfriend or boyfriend at the beginning of the season, "I'll see you after the season's over"? When you watch television, do you flip a basketball from hand to hand? When you ride your bike, do you dribble the ball alongside it? If you can't answer, "Yes," to most of these questions, stop kidding yourself about becoming a pro. It's fun to fantasize, but remember that that is what you're doing.

If you do make the all-out effort described above, and if all you've read about your chances so far hasn't changed your mind in the slightest about your pro plans, then stick to your dream. You *could* make it. A few do, every year.

If you aren't so sure the NBA is part of your future, don't give up on the game. Examine the options. Thousands of people are actively involved with basketball on other levels. The odds of finding some spot in basketball aren't bad at all. In fact, it's a sure bet that you can do so.

For players, many avenues are open, from pickup games in the city park to well-organized YMCA leagues or even semipro ball. Whatever your skill level, you can get into a game somewhere if you want to. Various organizations, such as JayCees, have teams, leagues, and even state tournaments, so that members can continue to play into their thirties. Churches often sponsor teams and form leagues with other church teams so that players can participate for as long as they feel able.

If it is not playing you crave so much as the excitement of association with pro athletes and being at pro games as an insider, you might consider becoming a team doctor, trainer, or one of the assistant coaches. If you don't mind the lack of job security (team owners are prone to dismiss a coach after one or two losing seasons), you can even become a head coach if you work your way up from high school jobs and then through the college ranks, especially if you do become a top-rated college player.

Finally, consider the wide-open field of high school coaching, which may be an end in itself rather than a step on the way to becoming a college or pro basketball coach. Coaching has been pictured in many ways. Coaches who have left the field early and are disillusioned with their old jobs may paint a gloomy picture: administrative pressure to produce winners; players who have talent but break training; players who have talent and get appendicitis or break an ankle at tournament time; players who have talent and don't even try out for the team; marriages pushed to the breaking point by the coach's long hours away from home; heartbreaking losses, humiliating losses, and seemingly endless losses.

I've coached for a number of years, and I'm nowhere near burning out or giving up. I've experienced many of the things that drive coaches from the field. I think it's worth it. One benefit is closeness to the game of basketball. It's a wonderful, complex, ever-changing game, a physical chess game, a challenging sport that is just downright great fun. Then there are the players. Sure, some talent is wasted, misspent, unused. But what about the talent that is hidden until you find it within some youngster, growing like a fragile bloom in a far corner of the meadow? You take that bloom, guard it, nurture it, watch it grow healthier and stronger and better—and you know joy. The untalented players are also worth it, too, every one of them. I love to be around them all, to share with them and to lead them. That privilege is, to me and to most of the coaches I know, a sacred and significant one.

For every negative aspect of the job, coaching brings many positives. Overcoming odds, winning games against bigger or higher-ranked schools, seeing players you've coached named all-state players or getting scholarships to good colleges, and eventually seeing some become good coaches or, better yet, good citizens—yes, the rewards are there.

Whatever your choice of jobs, you want to be the best player you can be. You want to help the team, honor the school, make your family proud, be with the friends who are on the squad, get into top condition, feel the thrill of competition, and find out what your capabilities are. This book will help you reach those goals.

chapter two

what is your coach looking for?

It's the first practice. You're raring to go, but you feel a bit nervous. You're standing in a line with a whole cornrow of guys, many of whom look confident, big, well-built. Rumors have been flying about the coach's likely picks and cuts. So-and-so has it made—he's the banker's son. The skinny guy at the end of the line was leading scorer last year on the junior varsity team; he'll make the cut. The coach always did like the freckle-faced kid next to you, so he's a cinch to make it, too. And so on.

Then there is your own case. You, the unknown, the one who feels awkward when he gets nervous, who falls down a lot when he's trying to look good. You, who tries to look tall but is stuck next to a 6′7″ beanpole the first day so your 5′8″ looks like 5′2″. What are your chances?

Whether you fit the above description or you *are* the banker's son, the JV star, the freckle-faced kid, or the beanpole, there are many ways to improve your chances greatly.

Get rid of the notion that a coach plays athletes whose parents have influence or because they were decent athletes in the past, or because he likes them more than some of the others. That's nonsense! After all, every self-respecting coach wants as good a team as he can have. Doesn't it follow, then, that he will pick and play athletes who can do the best job?

If self-esteem were always based on doing one's best and not on such things as exhibiting raw physical ability, most of the ill feelings that arise from being cut or getting too little playing time would never develop. If, in spite of everything you do, you *are* cut or you *don't* get that starting assignment, remember that you deserve as much respect as anyone else, as long as you gave it your best shot. You aren't responsible for your natural ability, so you might as well learn to live with whatever you—and the other players—have.

None of this philosophizing excuses you from doing all you can to enhance your abilities. Nor does it stop you from doing some things that may compensate for physical disadvantages.

First, listen carefully to everything the coach says. He will appreciate it, and he will observe that you are eager to learn. He may tell the players who are trying out what he is looking for. Believe him! He has no reason to lie about what he wants from his players.

Second, *hustle*. Hustling will make up for many mistakes. Don't ever stand around flat-footed in practice. Give it your all. Any coach can see and appreciate a 100% effort, and every coach wants it. You will also have a conditioning edge over players who coast whenever they can. Even if the coach isn't watching you, work hard. He'll see you a number of times when you don't think he's looking.

Third, show a good attitude. That means you never second-guess the coach, though you may, when the time is right, ask for a fuller explanation of something you don't understand. Also, don't gripe or moan about drills, don't sulk when you're left sitting during parts of the scrimmages, and don't bellyache about getting hurt every time there's contact on a play. *Never* criticize other players. If you try to make someone else look bad, you may succeed, but you won't make

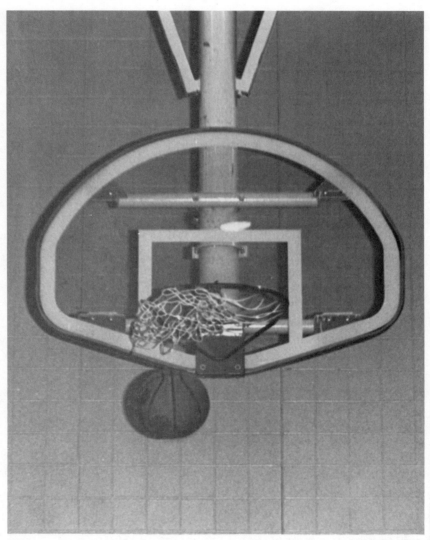

When all is said and done, this is what counts in a basketball game—learn to make it happen!

yourself look good, and very soon other people will catch on to what you're doing and assume you must be falling short of the mark since you have a need to hide behind criticism. Don't let a jammed finger or mild ankle twist sideline you, but never take a chance with a genuinely serious or potentially serious injury, or you may end your whole season or career. Don't forget to encourage others and give them credit when it's due for a good effort, an assist, or putting a good move on you.

Fourth, be obedient. Abide by every rule. Whether you agree with every rule or not is irrelevant. Obey them all. Follow all the training rules, the rules about what you wear to practice, and the rules on when you should be on the court for practice (the earlier the better). Obey the rules concerning how to run a play. For instance, if last year's coach told you to block out and keep the man out on a rebound, and this year's coach says to make contact and then go immediately after the ball, do it the way this year's coach says he wants it done. Both rebounding methods are correct, so it's simply a matter of coaching preference. Also abide by rules of form. Even if you think you shoot better your old way, use the way you're told is correct. Sometimes practicing the wrong way for a long time results in better shooting than using correct form does at first. In the long run, however, the right way will lead to more improvement. In addition to following the rules, obedience means being at every practice. Don't delude yourself that an excusable absence won't affect the coach's assessment of you as a player. After enough excused absences, your seriousness about the game will be questioned, and you will probably be placed behind a player of equal ability who has faithfully attended practices and games.

Fifth, be heard. The coach is human. If you're quiet and shy, he may not notice you as much as the ones who express themselves. Just be careful about *how* you're heard! Certainly, swearing, telling the coach how to do his job, and bragging are not the ways to make yourself noticeable. You can be heard out on the court, yelling cheerily to teammates, uplifting them without getting silly, shouting such things as, "Let's go!" when ready to start a drill and "Fire up, gang!" when the practice tempo is dragging. Coaches need and search for enthusiastic players. In both games and practices, tempo is a crucial concern. When a team's pace quickens, it often does better, partly because of the adrenalin that is infused into the players' systems. In practice, tempo is important because, without it, the players practice at a pace different from their game pace, so when they try to push harder in a game they find themselves in unfamiliar territory and make mistakes that only add to their shakiness.

One note for the enthusiast, however: when that coach's whistle blows, remember to be quiet and listen! That is not the time for hoopla.

Finally, the most significant method of all for attracting the notice of a coach and insuring that you'll get into games is to become a shooter. The simple fact is that no coach can keep a shooter on the bench forever. Coaches may not make much of that truth when giving team talks, but there's a good reason for that: everybody wants to score, and not many take a keen interest in defense, which is also crucial. However, a coach can make almost anyone who is sold on defense and is willing to work at it into a decent defensive player. A good shooter, on the other hand, must make himself good. This is done to some extent by using proper techniques, but the great shooter gets that way by shooting thousands and thousands of shots. If you really want to play, you must shoot all year-round.

This is an age of sports specialists. You can go out for every sport under the sun, but you'd better decide which is your main sport and concentrate on that one during the off-season. Basketball, in particular, requires that kind of concentrated effort. Only the very best football players work year-round, usually on weight training. Volleyball players may catch a clinic and, without much more than that, excel through seasonal practices alone. Not so in basketball, soccer, track, or gymnastics. Nor would it be possible to be a better-than-average performer in swimming or baseball without much off-season work.

You can't forget about basketball for nine months and then, with a burst of effort or overtime practice, turn into a good shooter. Shooting skills are fragile. They can fade temporarily even during the season, let alone with a nine-month layoff. Shooting practice does have one advantage over spiking a volleyball, pumping weights, or running laps: it's more fun, since you can vary it both physically and mentally (more on this subject later).

If you are determined to devote a large share of your time to basketball, refer often to the tips given in this book so that you will not just be practicing, but practicing correctly. As you work at the sport, you will know that your efforts are well worth the time spent on them for you will improve each day.

chapter three

set definite goals...and more

The preceding chapters have given you an indication of how tough it may be to make something of yourself in basketball. To do this you need self-motivation. Presumably, you have more than one reason for wanting to improve. List those reasons. When practice sessions seem to get longer and your enthusiasm begins to taper off, take your list out and look it over slowly and thoughtfully.

In addition to that list, make a list of goals. It is far more rewarding to put some perspiration into a long-term project if you reach a number of progressively more difficult goals en route. List your goals from immediate to long-range. Your immediate goals might include these:

Make the cut.
Shoot 5% better on practice free throws than last year.
Play every game.
Average three fouls or fewer each game.

Be a double-figure rebounder.
Make 100% effort every minute.

Some goals for farther down the road could include the following:

Be a starter.
Be a double-figure scorer.
Be the team's top rebounder.
Make all-conference.
Be the assist leader.
Shoot over 50% from the field.

Eventually, you could set goals such as these:

Earn a scholarship.
Be all-state.
Set a school rebounding record.
Start on a university team by sophomore year.
Coach a high school team.
Take a high school team to a state tournament.

You will, of course, want to modify these lists considerably so that each goal is commensurate with your own talents and expectations, as well as with your position and your team's style of play.

In addition to such goals, hang on to some of your fantasies. When you're daydreaming, there is nothing wrong with envisioning yourself reverse slam-dunking the ball to lead the Celtics to another NBA Championship. Just don't lose touch with reality! You have to come back to earth long enough to hear your coach, keep your studies up to date, and get along with your family.

Both fantasies and goals change for normal people. If the Phoenix Suns appeal to you next year more than the Celtics, you can be their star instead. Similarly, if circumstances change, your goals can be altered. If you have planned to be the team's top rebounder and a 6'11" junior transfers to your school, set a different goal or face frustration. If you planned to be a 50% shooter but discover you are halfway through the season and going at a 55% clip, reset your goal for next season to 60%. There is nothing magical about a goal, and you never need to be compulsive about reaching one. Goals are meant only to help, to guide, to provide a progress check, to give you something to look forward to through the daily grind.

Many young players will want to include in their list of goals the raising of the money needed to attend a clinic or two. The money is easier to come by when you start saving in September than if you wait until summer has started. Another goal you must set for yourself is to spend a certain number of hours shooting each day during the off-season. Be sensible in setting this goal; if it's too steep, you may give up on it entirely. Figure what your daily average will be, with a job and any other commitments figured into your plans. Once you set this goal, stick to it. Don't think you can let it slide for a week and then double up the next; you probably won't do so. Ruts are formed easily.

Decide what goals you wish to share with whom. Don't boast in general about what you plan to accomplish. You'll end up feeling unduly pressured and may chuck your goals in disgust, as well as in embarrassment. You'll want to tell some goals to a close friend, some to your parents, and some to no one.

If you aren't sure what some of your goals should be, talk to a knowledgeable person about your capabilities and potential. Your coach or an assistant coach may help you set goals and may invite you to some extra help sessions or suggest a particular clinic that can help you reach those goals. An older player, perhaps one who has graduated from your school, could be a source of advice. Big brothers and sisters also may make good counselors. Look around at others' performances. If there is someone on the team you consider close to you in ability, you may strike up a conversation in which you can ask that player what his hopes and expectations are. Often others feel flattered that you take such an interest in their feelings and future, as long as you don't come across as being nosy.

chapter four

be good to yourself

Lessons in first aid or treatment of athletic ailments are boring until you are the one who must give first aid or who has the ailment. Unless you are well educated in this area, your best bet is to *prevent* injuries.

In both prevention and treatment of injuries, common sense is the most vital ingredient. Exercise good sense in all that you do. You won't ever know how good you can be in basketball if you're sidelined after some needless horseplay or because you ignored some indications of impending ill health.

One health department in which you can exercise good judgment is the matter of smoking. You are young, and you may be able to smoke moderately without noticing any effect. Don't be deceived by this; the effects *are* there. You may still be able to run two miles; you never cough; you can run circles around some of your nonsmoking teammates. But have you ever thought that you might be still better if you didn't smoke? Has it occurred to you that by this time next year you might want to play ball as well or better than this year but find it more difficult?

To a great extent basketball success consists of getting an edge on the opposition. Little details overlooked here and there may seem insignificant but, when added up, often spell the difference between a winner and a loser. Take every edge—big or small—you can get if you want to be a winner.

Serious young athletes won't have problems with alcohol, cigarettes, or drugs. Yet they may find their performance diminished by other poor health habits. Beware of a diet of junk food; it will eventually sap your strength. Don't put off studying so you have to stay up late or get up too early; think ahead when you're tempted to waste a study hall. Remember that the night before an important game you may be excited and find it hard to get to sleep. Learn to wind down before bedtime by reading, playing a quiet game such as checkers, or relaxing in whatever way suits you best. When you go outside during cold weather, dress properly. It's not as much fun to play ball with a runny nose. If it's raining or you have just showered, wear something on your head when you go out.

Proper footwear is necessary. Make certain that your shoes are in good condition and fit properly. A worn tread can cause an unnecessary, bone-crunching spill or a muscle-tearing slip. Loose shoes can give you blisters, and no one plays best with a silver-dollar-sized blister on each foot. Wearing two pairs of socks during the preseason or longer may help.

Girls should be careful about the brand of tennis shoes they buy. Many girls buy boys' sizes and styles, which is a mistake in most cases, because the average girl's foot is narrower than the average boy's foot. With the modern-day increase in girls' athletic participation, more and more strictly girls' styles are becoming available.

The cost of basketball shoes may not be a true sign of their worth. Some brands are high-priced because of a successful sales history, which won't make your feet any more comfortable. Some more expensive brands may last a bit longer, but if you buy new shoes each year, you may not want to take that factor into account. The important things are fit, comfort, and support. Take your time in making a selection to be sure your choice is good.

Jogging shoes are not recommended for the gym. You will get best results from shoes with treads made for maneuvering on a hard, smooth surface. Jogging does not involve sudden lateral movement, so the tread requirements are not the same as for basketball.

While we're discussing shoes, I should remind you that your street shoes are also important. You can blister from them, too. Tight footwear can also lead to ingrown toenails, or at least aggravate them. You don't want to go onto the court with a supersensitive big toe and have a 200-pounder jump on it.

Shoes with poor support allow undue arch stress, and those who have weak arches may have problems with them. The bones and ligaments creating and supporting the arch of the human foot are complex and fragile. They need the protection of shoes with adequate support.

If you do twist an ankle, on or off the basketball court, examine it carefully to make sure it isn't serious. If it is a mild twist, walk it out right away. If it seems to be more than that, get an X-ray instead of risking further damage.

Once an ankle has been twisted, it is easy to twist it over and over again. If the twist was very mild, exercise and strengthen the ankle as soon as you are able. If it was more serious, have it wrapped for a week or two. During the off-season you can wrap it yourself. A simple method of wrapping an ankle without using an excessive amount of tape is diagrammed in the figure on page 22.

Again, prevention is better than cure. Get a jump rope and use it year-round. It will strengthen your ankles. Jogging on semisoft surfaces prevents another common problem, shinsplints. Coming into the gym and doing sprints and other drills on the hard floor without prior roadwork is inviting shin miseries. Some players, however, experience soreness in their leg bones no matter what they do; the common term for this is *growing pains*. If you've shot up two to six inches in the past few months, you may feel some of these pains. You'll outgrow them, but if they seem to get steadily worse,

Make sure the tape stays as smooth as possible to avoid chafing inside the shoe. You can use an underwrap next to the skin or keep your sock on as an underwrap.

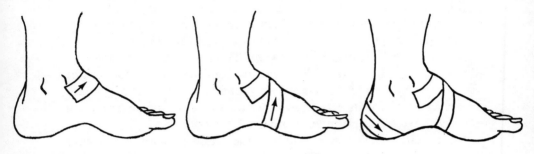

1. Start upward.

2. Wrap under the arch.

3. Follow the curve of the heel.

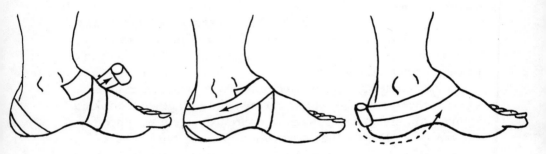

4. Wrap up to the center on the other side.

5. Wind across the ankle.

6. You will be following the curve of the heel on the other side next.

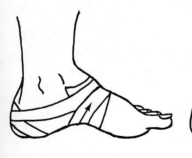
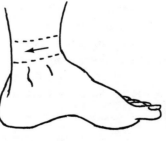

7. Bring it back up from the heel; tape is again on this side.

8. Wrap above the foot.

9. Finally, wrap it back again to lock it.

see a doctor anyway, just in case the cause of your discomfort is something else.

Protect your eyes. If you scrimmage with persons who let their fingernails grow too long, ask them to cut them. Also watch for jewelry on other players and remind them that these dangers should be removed. Be nice about it, but be firm—it's your vision that is threatened.

Get some bacterial spray and keep it in your gym bag for minor cuts and abrasions. Without prompt attention, infection could set in. Don't be overanxious; try to be casual and inconspicuous about little scrapes and your treatment of them. You never want to create an image of yourself as a marshmallow. Be matter-of-fact about personal first aid. Get back into action as quickly as possible. Don't bring up your aches and pains again once they are cared for.

If you have an injured leg or ankle, don't continue taping it too long. It will strengthen more speedily without tape. I have known athletes who had weak ankles for 10 years because they always taped them; their ankles magically recovered when they stopped using tape.

If you have an illness of any kind, be certain it is not serious before you play. Weakened health invites complications you don't want.

If you have any doubt about the extent of an injury or the seriousness of an illness, consult a physician.

chapter five

tricks of the trade

M any of the moves that will be discussed in this chapter and forthcoming chapters are difficult to execute. They will be explained and illustrated as simply as possible. Some of the moves may appear simple before you try them or look easy when you watch proficient players accomplish them, but don't be misled. Without much practice, you will not master them. Some, when first you try them, may even seem hopelessly hard. None of them are *that* tough, though. Keep at it, and suddenly you'll find them clicking.

GETTING OPEN

A major part of offensive basketball success hinges on a deceptively simple aspect of the game—*getting open*. No doubt, you've been told the primary basic of the art: come to the ball. Standing like a rock when a pass is sent your way guarantees interceptions. Of course, you could do even worse—turn your back to the ball.

Assuming you've played some type of organized basketball, you will be ready for most passes and will move quickly to insure a reception. But as your competition improves, you may soon find yourself in a situation where alertness and quick ball movement are just not enough. What do you do when a defensive player is denying that point-to-wing pass? Most team offenses are initiated with such a pass, and a determined denial of it can wreak havoc unless you have practiced some methods of freeing yourself.

The first instinct of a player who is subjected to good defensive pressure before a pass is to run away from the defender, trying to get space to make the pass a safe one. Such a tactic is a mistake. Try doing just the opposite: go *into* the defender, *then* jump quickly away (see photos below). Otherwise it's too easy for the defensive

Instead of running away from the defender to get open, go into him first.

It is then a simple matter to complete what is called a *square-out* by stepping quickly away for the pass.

player to stay with you. This does not mean you should push the defender away with the hand or forearm, though in the lane area a post person may have to do a little of that. Turn in toward the defender enough to get body contact, then go away.

Another maneuver, which is especially good if you are being called for too many fouls and don't want to risk an offensive foul call with the hit-and-run tactic described above, is to *circle* the defender (see page 27). Merely run a quick, tight circle right around him! If this has been done to you, you know it is disturbing to a defensive player, to say the least. There is no way to tell when the offensive player is going to break away, and it is hard to know when to stop following without losing your position in relation to the ball.

If, on a previous possession by your team, you found that the defender playing against you was ably denying you the ball, you may try starting farther in toward the baseline; then walk parallel to the free throw lane boundary with an arm out for the pass away from the side the defender is on. The defender can't risk overplaying the pass too far from such a position because you can easily backdoor him if he does. This move works well if you are being arm-guarded, i.e., the defender is attempting to deny you the pass with an arm between you and the ball rather than with the body. The photos on page 28 show what can happen if the defender does get the body out in front of you—you have an unobstructed route to the basket.

If you have succeeded once in backdooring the defense, the stage is set for an easy move—fake a backdoor effort and come immediately back toward the ball (see photos on page 29).

Remember that you have a big advantage on offense: you know in advance where you are going, and the defender doesn't. He must wait for your move, so you have a jump on him. Don't hold back. Make sharp moves; don't let a small hesitation allow a defensive recovery.

These ways of getting open are also applicable when the out-of-bounds pass is being denied. In most cases, they are equally good for a wing-to-baseline pass, once the baseline person has left the post spot and come out into open territory.

Here the defender is too well positioned to permit either a square-out or a backdoor attempt.

The offensive player reverses his direction and follows a circular path.

When the circle is completed the offensive player has good inside position on the defender.

When the defensive player is positioned too far behind the offensive man the offensive man should stay by the lane and signal for the pass on his safe side.

The backdoor play yields an easy score.

The defensive player can easily be beaten backdoor when he has taken his position too high.

Here the defender has fallen prey to a backdoor
play and is too eager.

Instead of continuing the movement backdoor, the
offensive man quickly reverses direction and is
ready for a pass in good scoring position with the
defender helpless behind him.

OFFENSIVE MOVES

Now that you've sprung loose from the defense and received the ball,
you may continue the regular offensive pattern, but *always look to
the basket first*. If you have an open shot from 12-15 feet away, most
coaches want the shot to go up. If you don't at least look toward the
hoop, you relieve the pressure on the defender. You're telling him
that there is one less option he has to worry about from you, and he
is doubly prepared to stop a pass.

If you are a respectable shot, there are a couple of things you can do to help you get that shot away. The first and simplest is to put the ball up without any hesitation. If, as in the photos on page 31, the defensive player is playing far enough away to make a forward step necessary before a block attempt, shoot at once, before or during that stride forward. The average player will let a slight hesitation destroy this golden opportunity. Get squared up the same as you would (hopefully) for any other shot than a defended lay-up. Failure to observe fundamentals like properly aligning your shoulders with the target ruins shooting percentages.

If the other team is zoning and your coach's emphasis is on rapid ball movement, you may be best advised to pass right away if the quick jumper isn't there. Against a man-to-man defense, and with some more deliberate zone offenses, you can try a jab step.

The jab step is a definite, swift forward step toward the defender. Most defensive players are trained to respond to a forward offensive movement by taking a retreat step. That way they prevent the offensive player from driving around. If the properly trained defensive player overdoes this retreat step, his balance is too far to the rear, however. In such a case, rock back immediately and get the shot off before the defender recovers (see photos on page 32).

Sometimes a defender will make an impulsive move in a different direction instead of taking a retreat step. If the movement is to either side, set the ball down and go around with a *crossover step* (see page 33). This consists of beating the defender by getting a foot past his leg on the side you are going by. If that side is opposite to the foot you used to jab step, as shown, you can take the crossover step before setting the ball down. But, if it's on the same side, you must get the ball down early to avoid a traveling violation.

If the defender's step was toward you instead of to one side, you have a choice of which side to drive around on. If you jabbed with your right foot and are able to handle going left (which you should be able to do if you work on your own enough), going to the left is your best route unless defensive help is waiting there, since you can take the crossover step without a risk of traveling.

Whatever way you choose to drive, don't neglect another very

The defender's position is not close enough to the ball.

The player with the ball should quickly get off the shot, because the defensive player must take a forward step before being in position to stop a shot.

The player with the ball executes a jab, or rocker, step.

If the defender rocks back, the player with the ball has an immediate advantage.

Again, the player should get a shot off quickly before the defender can recover to stop the shot.

Once again the offensive player jab-steps.

This time the defender has shifted balance in the direction of the jab step.

The offensive player now "locks" the defender by getting a foot past hers and going around quickly.

basic fundamental: keep the ball away from the defender. You must dribble with the far hand. If the defense finds you cannot use your left hand for a dribble, you'll be easy to shut off. All the defense must do if you're strictly a righty is to guard half the width of your body (overshift), namely your right side, and you will have nowhere to go. When you go with your coach or on your own to scout other teams, this is a characteristic to look for. Does the person you are

Many coaches teach this W method of awaiting and taking a pass; its advantage over a clapping type of hand position is that the palms are out and provide a surer surface area to stop the ball.

This over-under grip works even better for sure pass reception, especially if the pass is a poor one.

observing ever go left, and if so, how well? If that weakness is apparent, you will want to guard the player with an overshift.

If it is necessary for you to pass off because the defensive player is doing a good job, because you are outside your shooting range, because you spot a teammate closer to the basket, or because you are having shooting problems and it would be best according to your coach and you to get the ball to a teammate who is currently hotter, look at the basket first anyway. Then use any pass that you're sure will get there. The days are over when form was spelled out rigidly for each type of pass. Now basketball is so fast-paced and players are so innovative that the only rule of passing is to complete the pass safely. Use whatever fakes, twists, etc., will work for the particular situation at hand, and don't hold back. Deliver that pass crisply. Lazy passing will doom an offense.

Special techniques for post players will be detailed in the following chapter.

chapter six

post moves

If you are primarily a post player (and almost all players find themselves playing the post area at some time), don't feel overly dismayed when you are neglected. It often happens. For one thing, a coach is responsible for the entire team, and ordinarily a minority of them are post people. For another, the progress of a post player is often slower than the progress of players focusing on general ball-handling, passing, and shooting. Many coaches feel that their time yields the greatest results when spent on those general skills.

Whether your coach spends much time on post moves or not, don't neglect practicing them. They are hard enough after much practice, and without it you won't make many good moves at all. A post player goes up against the opposition's biggest, strongest players. A high percentage of post players are upperclassmen, who have grown taller through their school years and, when nearing graduation, are likely to have a height advantage over younger players. Besides all that, the post area is a dangerous area to the defensive team, because much of a good team's scoring comes from there. Statistics say that a winning team's pivot player receives the ball at least 10% more than does the pivot man on the losing side. Once the ball is inside, near the basket, breathing room becomes scarce— everybody is out to stop you.

Good post players usually follow a few simple, but not easy, procedures. Learn these until they become instinctive. Away from the lane, a player often can decide early what move he will make, but inside, the move is determined by how you are defensed at the moment you receive the ball, so you must act almost instinctively. Such rapid reactions stem from hours upon hours of practice. Truly superb post players often do not surface until well into their college career, because it takes a long time to make all the post moves second nature.

The player illustrates the spot and direction a post player should select early in the game; she is on the block facing into the lane.

First, come up court and line up on the high side of the box, facing into the lane. Just as the pass is coming from the point guard to a wing player, step toward the baseline and then pivot so that the defender is shut off behind you. Be sure you have your knees bent, taking up lots of space with your rump, and keep your elbows outward. Now receive the ball with your palms facing outward (away from you), not in a clapping position; you will find that the palms-out method gives you much surer receptions. When the ball comes, pull it into your chest, keeping those elbows out.

Once you have the ball, you must know where the defensive player is. If you can't feel him behind you, peek over your shoulder. His position decides what you must do:

1. If the defender is squarely behind you, use a turnaround jump shot or get the ball back outside quickly.
2. If the defender is playing less to the basket side of you than to the free throw line side, execute a baseline power slide for a score. This means you move in hard and low at the basket for a lay-up. If you set the ball down (never more than one bounce!) explode upward off both feet as you pick up the ball. *Hurl* yourself at the basket, so your arms will be up high enough when you release the shot to insure that you will make it even if you are fouled. If you have a good, confident stride, you can get a lay-up with no dribble and of course must go off your lead foot to avoid a travel call. Whichever way you do it, use the body as a shield between the ball and the defender. On this particular shot, squaring up (bringing the shoulder in line with the target on a pass or shot) is not the main consideration; protection is. Your back should be visible to someone on the other side of the lane from you (see pages 40–41).
3. If the defender is playing on the baseline side of you, step around on the high side, toward the circle, and get off a soft hook shot, as in the photos on page 42). On the shot, keep the nonshooting arm up so that, if you are fouled, that is the arm the opponent will hit, and you will have a better chance for a three-point play.

The position below the block has allowed the offensive player to step into the pass and still have excellent position as she receives the ball.

The defender has taken position too close to the baseline, so the offensive player posts up just below the block.

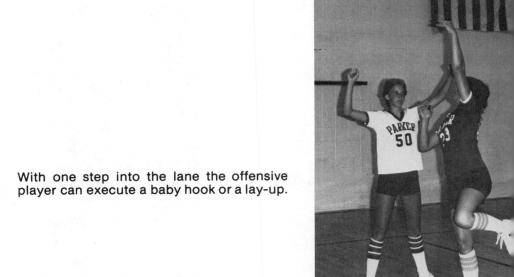

With one step into the lane the offensive player can execute a baby hook or a lay-up.

The defensive player has chosen a position on the high side of the block.

The offensive player steps out and takes the pass.

Now the defender's position allows the offensive player to slide underneath her along the baseline to get off a lay-up.

Even though another defensive player has come quickly across the lane to help out, the power slide is a high-percentage shot when the player executing it uses the correct hand and shields herself by keeping her body turned into the defensive player.

Here the defender (dark jersey) is positioned high but is still on the baseline side of the post player.

The post player steps around into the lane for the pass from the point or opposite wing.

An immediate shot should yield a score when the pass has been taken in such ideal position.

All the above moves are for a low post (a player on the offense or below the block) when you are not fronted. If the opponent does play between you and the ball, here is what to do:

1. Turn toward the lane enough so that your shoulders are between the defender's shoulder blades or, if you wish, so that your back is to the ball and your rump to the defender. When you do this, keep your arms up high and keep the hand nearest the defender *directly under your chin* (see pages 44–45). This will prevent you from being called for a pushing foul quite as often as if your hand was at the defender's back.
2. Now raise the hand farthest away from the defensive player, signaling that you are able to receive a pass.
3. Wait! Don't move away from the defensive man until the ball is over your head. Then take it with two hands (again preventing foul calls), while pushing the defender away with your backside.

As the game progresses, pay close attention to how the defensive player is positioning himself. If you find he is always directly behind, stay on the box as a low post. If he is below the box, overguarding the baseline move, position yourself on the baseline side of the box next time up court, giving yourself a closer shot when you take the ball, and step into the lane on the high side (see page 46). If he is always on the high side, come up to the next free throw mark; this gives you plenty of room for your power slide along the baseline (see page 46). If you are fronted every time, post up a step out from the lane, giving yourself more room on the backdoor pass.

If you are sandwiched between two opponents (which, by the way, is a compliment to you, because no one double-teams a weak player!), you can try moving up to a middle post position, halfway between the block and the free throw line (see photo on page 47). If you receive the ball in this position, your best move is to execute a *reverse* pivot (swing around by dropping a foot back, not bringing a foot around in front) so that you are squared up the basket. Before you make this pivot, fake in the direction opposite your

Now the post player is being fronted.

The post player has a hand, palm down, under her chin, elbow out to take up room, and a hip and shoulder against the defensive player; she signals with the other hand for a backdoor pass.

As the ball comes, the post player should hold her position to keep the defensive player out.

Notice that the ball is past a point over her head before the post player jumps into the lane to take it for an easy score.

As she jumps to the ball and takes it with both hands, the post player has now left the defensive player helpless against a close-in shot.

Because the post player (dark jersey) was positioned at the free throw lane mark above the block (since the defender was on that side of the block), she now has ample room to go in underneath for a lay-up.

The post player is being sandwiched (double-teamed), so she takes a position two free throw lane marks above the block, allowing much more room for movement.

The post player is again double-teamed and has positioned herself at the free throw line, again allowing ample room for movement toward the basket.

pivot direction, but make the fake with the head and shoulders only; do not move your feet. If you do, you eliminate one of the pivot possibilities because you must use the foot still planted as a pivot foot; many post men travel because of a foot fake.

Once you have squared up properly, you can do several different things: take the jump shot, fake and go opposite with a crossover step or one dribble, or pivot back again for a pass back out.

Finally, you may wish to move into the lane or out along the baseline to get a pass. If you pop out along the baseline and receive the ball, you want to get a baseline drive if at all possible. Remember that, if there is contact, the odds are against the defender on the foul call, so if you have any room at all for a baseline drive, don't hesitate.

If you are on the side of the lane away from the route of the ball, and you have decided to flash-cut into the lane, try to pivot on your inside (basket-side) foot and swing around toward the basket with the other foot to get yourself as close as you can for a lay-up or a baby hook shot.

You need to practice each of these moves a great deal or you will never feel confident enough to use most of them in games. It is one thing to understand what you should do, and another thing to do it with aggressiveness. If a post player must have one characteristic for success, it is aggressiveness. It is a bruising, thumping, elbowing, pushing, shoving fight underneath the basket. Timid souls weren't meant to post up!

chapter seven

make your weak hand strong

Players who can dribble to their left or right and who can shoot as accurately after a drive in either direction have a big edge on those who can go only one way. The advantage is half a step on the defense, usually the difference between being stopped and being able to drive around to get open.

The half-step difference comes because the defensive player cannot overplay you to the strong-hand side if he knows you are a threat both ways. If the defensive player must play you straight away, you have that half-step, whichever side you choose to go on, and after a good fake you can break around. If the defensive player assumes you can go in only one direction with the ball when you can actually go both ways, you have a decided advantage until he wises up. In fact, you have a full-step advantage one way. He will be overguarding you on one side and leaving the other open for a quick move.

The sad thing is that few younger players are concerned about developing the weaker hand. Even when they recognize their need for it, they often put off working on it until it's too late and others on their team have surpassed them. The few players who use both hands are generally forced to do so because at one time their good hand was injured. A few others are blessed with ambidexterity.

Consistently favoring one hand leads to a decided difference between how you use one hand and how you use the other. You now face the dilemma everyone must settle: in order to develop that other hand, you must be willing to look bad for a while. The only other alternative is doubling your efforts in the off-season when practicing alone. If you always practice with friends or a family member, it's tempting to go ahead and use your better hand in order to perform well at the moment.

What it all boils down to is that you must pay the price now or pay it later. You can use that weaker hand when scrimmaging *from now on,* knowing you'll throw the ball away a few times and feel foolish but that the day will come when you'll be a tougher offensive player to stop. Or you can be comfortable right now, avoiding the risk of looking incompetent, making only right-hand moves so you can score *today,* and knowing that around the corner are some good defensive players who will shut you off and maybe even spoil your chances to play college ball.

There are some things you can do to get through the awkward stages more quickly. The most effective method is to do a little extra practicing. Don't give up your scrimmage time with friends, but sneak in a few extra minutes every day on your own for strictly weak-hand work. Do all the ball-handling drills in Chapter 15 of this book. Don't stop with that, though. Shoot those left-handed hooks and lay-ups until they're down pat.

Here's another secret to getting comfortable in game situations with that weak hand. Whenever you are bringing the ball up court, if there is no press, bring it up left-handed (or right-handed if you are a lefty). This gives you that many more minutes of left-handed dribbling during actual play, and it allows you to continue left or switch and drive right, either of which is a little easier than switching and then going left.

A great deal of ball-handling skill is based on your confidence. Be patient with yourself and be assured that you will become proficient with your weak hand. Don't let a goof here and there discourage you. Every mistake is a learning experience that takes you one step closer to your goal! You can figure that you have a certain number of slips to make as advance payment for future greatness.

Another valid tip for you to consider: if you're working out regularly with persons who, like yourself, want to become as good as they can be, challenge them now and then to a left-handed scrimmage. You can do this in several different ways: (1) You can handle the ball only with the left hand. (2) You can shoot lay-ups only with the left hand. (3) You can use the right hand but cannot score unless you have also used the left hand before the shot goes up. (4) You can use either hand, but a score off a drive to the left or from a left-handed shot is worth an extra point. If you do this, you need not fear looking any worse than your buddies, having stuck them with the same handicap.

One last piece of advice: if you're planning to use your weak hand during a game but aren't totally convinced that it's one of your better moves, it doesn't hurt to mention casually to your coach that you're trying to go left (or right) more. Don't overdo it with dire predictions that you will look awful for a game or two; just let him know what you are doing, thus increasing the odds that he will overlook some early mistakes instead of wondering what suddenly happened to your expertise on the court.

chapter eight

make yourself quicker

It is generally accepted that a player is either quick or he isn't. If he isn't, this thinking goes, he probably never will be; if anything, he will get a little slower as he matures. Don't subscribe to such nonsense! You can be quick even if you don't think you are now, and if you are already quick, you can probably become quicker still.

Players simply do not realize that, as with most physical skills, quickness can actually be *practiced*. Those who are quick are those who have practiced being quick, whether knowingly or unknowingly. Just as using strength makes your muscles stronger, exercising quickness makes your body quicker.

Do not confuse quickness with raw speed. There may always be teammates who can run faster than you in a 100-meter dash. That ability is almost trivial on a basketball court. You will rarely have to run more than 20 yards at a time, going full speed on a basketball floor.

Have you ever given someone a head start of even two or three yards and then tried to catch him? It's seldom easy, and in 20 yards it's usually impossible. That means your starting quickness matters more in a game than your raw speed ever could.

Here are some facts you may not know.

1. You are quick if you think you are.
2. If the opponent thinks you are quick, you're quicker.
3. No one is quick while setting the ball down (the first bounce of a dribble).
4. Quickness is relative only, never constant.
5. Childhood habits and the games you played determine most of your quickness or lack of it.
6. Quickness is often judged on skills that are not really related to quickness. Develop those skills, and you will appear to be far quicker.

Let's take a look at each of the statements you've just read and see how each works. The first is true because self-confidence and its product, aggressiveness, are integral parts of overall quickness. The opposite of this fact is the old adage, "He who hesitates is lost." *Making an unhesitating move* will help you be quick.

You must do two things to rid yourself of hesitation: (a) picture yourself as lightning-quick (you must believe it, because it's going to be so); (b) practice moves you need for games until you can do them smoothly and consistently (being smooth and making the move enough times will give you faith that you can do it).

The second statement works on the same principle as the first, but in reverse. When you convince someone going up against you that you are quick, that person will be more hesitant, primarily because he will be more tense. The longer he plays against you and the more moves you put on him, the more convinced he will become that he can't stop you, and the quicker you will seem to him. Therefore, when you have the moves and opportunity to make them, seize the chance and convince that foe!

The third statement is based on the laws of physics. It takes a certain amount of time to pick up a dribble and do something with it, so that's another moment of relative slowness. What this means is that defensively you should always be quicker than even a very quick opponent at certain moments, so capitalize on those moments. Be a defensive tiger, coming at your opponent furiously right then, and press your advantage.

The fourth statement, means that you face a wide range of playing situations. If you are facing an opponent who thinks he is slow, you will be relatively quick. If you are fresh in the game against a player who is bordering on exhaustion, you will be quicker than he is. If you are the recipient of a lazy pass, another team's player may look quicker than he is because he can take that pass away. Or, if you are a player who comes to meet the pass, you may make the would-be thief look slower than he is. After halftime, players who have kept moving and kept their heart rate going strong are a little quicker than the ones who collapse in a heap in the locker room while listening to the coach. All these variables of quickness add up, and they mean that you will have plenty of times when you can demonstrate quickness relative to your opponent's.

The fifth statement, explains why certain players are almost always quicker than others. Those children who participate heavily in rough-and-tumble games tend to be more aggressive and quicker ballplayers.

Finally, it was stated that developing skills not really related to quickness creates an appearance of quickness. Hustle is the clearest example. The player who goes all-out is always going to look quicker than the one who hangs back. Second effort, a favorite sermon topic of most coaches, is also guaranteed to make you look quicker. Hang on and keep getting back into the fray. I tell players to take it for granted that any loose ball is theirs and to go for it, not just once but for as long as it remains loose. I've seen third and fourth efforts result in ball possession, and I've seen players look mighty foolish when the ball came their way and they didn't even know it because they turned away after a token first effort.

Anticipation is another skill that makes you look quick. In a pressing situation I far prefer a good anticipator in a key spot than the quicker player who waits too long to get going. Be ready. Alertness is a great help.

Desire is yet another quickness-simulating trait. On defense it is the single most important characteristic. The best defensive player on the team may not be the quickest, but you can bet your game socks he's the one who *wants* to play defense.

Guts makes you quick, too. When you're in that second overtime and your tongue feels like a feather pillow and your legs feel like bricks, your personal courage alone will be the deciding factor in how hard you continue to move around the court. Make up your mind right now that you will have that courage.

There is also an art that determines quickness, called *moving your feet*. Don't stand flat-footed on defense for an instant! You can get from where you are to where you want to go much more quickly if your feet are already in gear than you can from a standing start. It's easy to neglect that little premise in practice, and those who do have cause to regret it.

As you can see from all these facts, you are not hopelessly confined to being slow. Today, you are on your way to being a quick ballplayer. Decide it; believe it; *be* it.

chapter nine

clumsy?

Clumsiness is a serious but common ailment that affects many tall players. Some of the shorter folks may also have a degree of clumsiness, but fewer of them do.

If you are tall and think you are uncoordinated, take heart. At least you aren't alone. I cringe to think of how many tall students are sitting in study halls because they believe themselves too clumsy to play ball. They are avoiding the one chief cure—athletic involvement. Sufficient repetition of muscle-coordinated movements eventually overcomes almost all lack of coordination.

If you have coordination problems, the best thing to do is to become active right away and to stay active in as many sports as possible. Play tennis, badminton, racquetball, handball, horseshoes, hopscotch, *anything*! But get right in there and participate anytime a game's afoot. Don't worry about being laughed at; you're paying your dues, and you'll have the last laugh. Otherwise, you risk being awkward permanently.

Your self-image is very important. When you picture yourself as a tall, stoop-shouldered, gangly Ichabod Crane type, you tend to stumble around and carry yourself poorly. Form a new image of yourself. You are now secretly *The Cat*. You are the smoothest, most powerful, most graceful person in the country. You move easily, effortlessly, like a panther. It doesn't matter if this is just a day-dream at first. Try this method, use it continually as you move around, and watch your dream come true.

The mind actually has the power to make the body actualize thought. In other words, "as a man thinketh in his heart, so is he." (Proverbs 23:7). Your body has a tendency to fulfill whatever ideal your brain creates for it.

If you have a cat or are around one, watch it closely. Study the way it moves, how it stretches, how it turns, how it jumps, and the way it cushions its landing with its feet. Watching this graceful creature helps you develop that image of smoothness for yourself. Humans are born imitators.

Dancing is an activity that helps improve coordination. You can put on a record at home and dance with Mom or Sis, or alone.

Any act requiring balance is beneficial to coordination. Walking along a railroad track is a common and useful pastime. You can balance on many other places, too, such as ledges here and there or school balance beams. Of course, be sure to exercise caution in any balancing exercise.

Make friends with a guard. Short, quick guards are generally better-coordinated than the big players, and spending time with them gives you a chance to imitate the characteristics that contribute to their gracefulness.

Practice all the ball-handling drills that guards use. These will improve your agility and quickness, and you will need ball-handling ability later, in most cases, to play college ball. Not only does an inside man need more general skill to make the grade on the tougher college level of competition, but many of the kids who were tall enough at 6'2" or so to play inside in high school ball will be converted to a guard spot or be cut at that height in college.

AGILITY DRILLS

Here are some agility drills to help accelerate your development.

The W

Put a piece of tape on the floor at five spots where the points of a W would be, each about 30 inches apart. Then, with feet together, jump from one point to the next, twisting around so you always land with your back to the next taped spot. After going through the W 10 times in this way, jump so you land backward, *facing* the next target spot, which you will land on backward after twisting. Finally, you can go through the W in a rapid-fire pattern, with no twists, alternately jumping forward and backward as swiftly as you can.

Tapping Drill

With two hands, flip the ball against a spot on the bangboard, catching it again in the air off a jump and flipping it back again *before* coming down. Thus you do a catch and a flip in midair off every jump. After 10 flip-ups, put the ball into the basket. Then go through the drill one-handed, first right and then left. Finally, repeat all three stages (two hands, right hand, left hand) from the other side of the basket. The drill is excellent for your timing, jumping, coordination, and as a tip-in drill. It also helps you learn to keep your arms up for rebounding, as discussed in Chapter 12.

Superman Drill

This is a standard drill used by most big men to perfect lay-ups and timing as well as to stay in condition. Take position at an angle to the bangboard and *outside* the lane. Jump-shoot the ball at a spot on the board that will cause it to carom off to the opposite side hard enough so that you will catch it and come down just outside the lane again, but on the other side. Pivot, jump-shoot back the other way, and keep going until you have 10 successful rebounds outside the lane.

Mikan Drill

This drill, named after George Mikan, a hardworking pivot man who did much to make pivot play a science, is now the most frequently used big man drill in basketball. It consists of making 10 consecutive lay-ups on alternate sides of the basket without allowing the ball to touch the floor. The drill may be executed in two basic forms: simply crossing back and forth underneath, making the lay-ups rapidly; or starting with your back to the basket, making a lay-up off a 180-degree midair twist, taking the ball as it comes through, pivoting around so your back is again to the basket (now on the other side), and continuing with another 180-degree lay-up.

One-Dribble Lay-ups

This drill can be fun. Start at the free throw line (see Glossary). Make a lay-up, allowing the ball to hit the floor only once. It will probably be easy from this distance. After repeating with a left-handed lay-up on the other side, take a step back from where you first started and try again. Keep backing up to see how far you can go. It is possible to make a lay-up with only one bounce from the midcourt line of a regulation-sized basketball court! It will seem impossible at first, but it isn't. I know a 5'10" athlete who can do it (not a pro or even a college star!).

Wall Whirls

This becomes the easiest of all the drills once you have done it a few times. Stand six feet away from a wall. Throw a two-handed chest pass against the wall at eye level, spin quickly, and catch the ball as it comes back to you, before it hits the floor. As you get quicker, pass the ball a little harder.

A last word for tall players: do not give up easily. It is a fact of life that taller players hit their peak later. Their height alone may carry them in grade school and sometimes in high school. But they will not be at their best as players until after many more months of practicing than are needed for shorter players to reach their physical peak. Staying active and continuing to work on agility and smoothness will guarantee that, sooner or later, you *will* become just as silky-smooth as anyone else.

If you are one who has always been physically active and whose growth came fairly evenly instead of in sudden spurts, you may never know what it is to feel awkward. Rather, you probably kept adjusting to your new height as it came about. That's the best way, but if you didn't do it that way, start now. Putting off coordination work will make progress slower and harder when you do start.

chapter ten

too small?

If you think lack of height is a disadvantage in basketball, you're right. If you think it's enough to prevent a player from making the team, you're wrong.

A shorter player has a few advantages, as a matter of fact. As mentioned in the preceding chapter, they are less likely to have coordination problems. A shorter player has not had to relearn body control after drastic changes in anatomical structure. If a player has always been shorter than his peers, he has probably learned little compensatory tricks to make him shiftier, better at faking people out. Finally, he is likely to be quicker than the taller player. One of the ways in which these various advantages help is shooting. The taller player's percentages may be better, since he's taking his shots from the lane, but it's most likely that the short player can outshoot the big man from 20 or 30 feet out and is also more accurate on a lay-up when coming full charge at the hoop on a fast break.

If you are small, there are some things you must do to insure

Lack of height is no excuse for lack of achievement. The all-state player in this photograph is the little 5'2" guard, Number 10.

success. First, outhustle the tall player. The big person is likely to tire more quickly. As the game progresses, you may find your quickness differential increasing drastically. You will be able to get the ball often by hustling after it. You can always maintain a good defensive position on that bigger person, and you should be able to make some moves to leave him in the dust when you want to. The height difference doesn't mean anything when you have the ball between the bigger defender and the basket!

Second, unless you are instructed to release from offense to stop the other team's fast break after a shot goes up, you must follow your shots. If you follow a shot quickly and unhesitatingly, you will often find you have inside position on the big guys, which will make them look foolish.

Third, learn to make up for a natural rebounding disadvantage by using proper technique. Rebounding is discussed in Chapter 12. Your positioning, where you go when you move in, and whether or not you keep your arms up before the rebound, will all determine how effective you are, whatever your size.

Fourth, be aggressive. You can intimidate a bigger player if you want to. Let him find out you are solid and not fun to collide with. If you're going for the ball, don't hold back. If you are going to make contact anyway, make it memorable to that big guy! Also be aggressive about butting around and elbowing in for a better position. When watching a game, instead of always concentrating on the guards, sometimes watch those inside men work. Learn to do some of the things they do.

Fifth, increase your jumping ability. Unless you work faithfully on this, it will do no good. You must get out that jump rope and go at it. Also go out for track. The following chapter discusses several methods of improving your jump so that you can surprise some big people in a jump ball situation. Or you can take a rebound away from the tall players when they stand flat-footed waiting for it. (Few bigger men really jump much on a rebound; they reach, tiptoe, or hop just a bit, but they don't have the time to explode upward like you do.)

The smaller player can successfully obscure the shooter's shot angle by getting a hand up over the shooter's forehead (*not* at eye level—that allows the shooter to look up over the hand).

In the *spider dribble* the player uses the hands alternately in front of and behind the body.

Sixth, be cool against the press. This is an important and useful skill that will make you as valuable in breaking a press as any big man could be. A press is rarely broken by fancy footwork or raw speed (the exception is a man-to-man press, which a good ball handler can wreck singlehandedly). Clean execution is required to break most presses. You must not panic—that's when the poor pass results in a turnover. Also, panic and fear blind you; you can see much more of what is developing and who is open if you concentrate on poise. Remember, anytime you have two people coming at you, someone on your side must be open; so don't just toss the ball up for grabs—take that moment to find the open man.

Seventh, work hard during the off-season to develop that outside shot. Know where you are likely to get a shot off in a game situation and concentrate on those areas. Read Chapter 13 for details on shooting.

If you fail to make the team, it's not because you are too small. It's because you were not willing to pay the necessary price in sweat and time to overcome the difference between your ability and that of the players who make it.

chapter eleven

increase your jump

You can measure your jump by what is called *jump differential*. This is the difference between your flat-footed reach and the point you can touch by jumping without a run. Stand next to a wall and reach up with a piece of tape. After sticking the tape as high on the wall as you are able without tiptoeing, take another tape and with one step or no steps jump as high as you can and slap this second tape onto the wall. Now get a bench or chair and a yardstick or tape measure and measure the distance between the tapes. That distance is your jump differential.

If your jump differential is 14-17 inches, you are average for a girl. For a boy, the average runs about two inches higher, in the range of 16-19 inches. A girl who has over a 20-inch jump differential or a boy who has over a 23-inch differential is an outstanding leaper. On the other hand, any girl with a differential under 12 inches, and any boy with one under 14 inches, probably lacks muscle tone and coordination and should get to work immediately on jumping rope and working on weights with the legs.

If your school has a leaper machine, you will have a fine opportunity to increase your jump by two to eight inches (some advertisers claim even more, but I have yet to see any results over eight inches). Just make certain you use the machine properly. Otherwise you can strain muscles, especially those in your shoulders and lower back. Read the directions for using the machine and follow them exactly.

An important point about using the leaper or any other method for increasing your jump: if you do not work regularly on it, it is pointless to do it at all. The gain will be nil or minimal at best. Steadiness and perseverance will reap dividends worthwhile to you.

Keep a tape up in your room or make a pencil mark somewhere inconspicuous so you can periodically check your progress by jumping beyond the spot you originally mark as your best height. It's fun to see yourself rabbiting upward, setting new records for yourself. Just don't check on your progress more often than weekly. You'll see the results you're after more clearly if you allow time for some improvement between checks.

For increasing your jump, the next best thing to a leaper, which many coaches believe isn't worthwhile because of injury risks, is a jump rope. The jump rope has the added advantage of helping with your coordination. Every serious player should have his own jump rope. I recommend thick nylon, not the ropes with plastic casing, because the hard plastic hurts when you miss, and ropes that aren't thick enough don't come around fast enough when you start increasing your speed.

Start with however many jumps you can do without getting totally exhausted; use jumps off both feet and then just left and just right. Make your jumping continuous and rapid. You may wish to gauge your workout by time rather than by number of jumps if you have trouble keeping count or have a clock within sight of your jumping area.

Each day, increase the number of each of the three types of jump (two feet, left, right) by 50, until you reach 300 of each. If you go by time, increase the time by one minute each day until you reach 10 minutes, making sure during that time that you use all three types of jump equally.

After you have hit the desired amount, add some doubles to your workout. Even if you just can't get the jump rope around twice before coming back down, assign yourself 25 attempts and make that many tries. Before long, you will find you can do it. When you succeed, try doubles off each foot, separately.

If you can hit the backboard, keep track of where you reach on it. Each day, reach at least that height 50 times. If you can hit the rim, do so, but don't hang on it. If you can stuff the basketball, do that 50 times instead. Some may not be able to stuff a basketball but can dunk a smaller ball—a volleyball, rubber ball, or tennis ball. Start with the smaller ball and after enough tries you may graduate to a larger one.

Simply standing in one spot and jumping off one foot 25 times, and then the other is good jumping work. Rest one minute between the pairs of 25 and repeat the set until you have done it 10 times. Just be careful if you start on a hard surface; make certain your shoes have enough cushioning or else start on a softer base for a time, or you could develop shinsplints and other problems.

Girls only: be aware that special bras are manufactured for female athletes. This type of bra may preserve some of your muscle elasticity, or uplift, and could spare some of you from discomfort during workouts.

Jumping ability or no, you should strive in all games and scrimmages to maintain the best possible position for rebounds and remember to keep your arms up in the lane area at all times, whether on defense or in anticipation of a defensive or offensive rebound. Take every little advantage you can grab, if you expect to win.

WEIGHT-LIFTING EXERCISES

If you, a family member, or your school has a set of weights, you can do the exercises below. Just make certain before and after doing these that you stretch out thoroughly. Failure to stretch out before you work on weights can invite a muscle pull or tear. Failure to work out the kinks with some stretching afterward may cause muscle spasms, charley horses, and reduced quickness and agility.

Clean and Press

Hold the bar in front of you with arms extended downward and palms toward you. With one swift motion and a slight dip of the body, yank the barbell up to the upper chest area. Then, in the second motion, extend the arms upward overhead. *Do not bend the knees and lean backward much or you can injure yourself.* Repeat 10-20 times; if you go over 10, rest between sets of 10.

Rowing

Grab the bar with the palms downward and less than a foot apart. Take the barbell from the floor to your upper thigh area by lifting with your legs until you are in a standing position (*keep your back straight*). Now do your rowing by simply lowering and raising the arms and shoulders only, very slowly, until you complete 20 circular movements.

Heel Raises

With the barbell resting on your shoulders behind the head and neck and palms upward, rise slowly to your toes, then sink down again (to a standing position). Repeat 50 times.

Straight Lift or Dead Lift with Legs

This is not recommended for players with knee problems, especially females who in general have weaker ligament structures than males. The exercise is nothing more than knee bends with a barbell. Set the barbell on the floor, then lift with the legs only by standing upright; go back down slowly and repeat 20 times.

All the exercises above will increase your jump. Even the rowing exercise, which is done with the upper torso, aids your jumping because much more of your jumping prowess than you may realize is dependent on the lift provided by the arms and shoulders.

Other exercises may be provided by your coach or the wrestling or football coach. The amount of weight you should use varies with your particular body weight, type, and strength. If you cannot get anyone to help you start with the correct amount of weight, remember that many repetitions with lesser amounts of weight are better for your overall conditioning and strength without adding unwieldy muscle bulk. You can establish an approximate weight to work with by first determining about how much you can lift on each exercise, then lifting 50-60% of that amount.

chapter twelve

get the rebound!

S ome characteristics you shouldn't exhibit in ordinary situations can be channeled very successfully into rebounding skills.

Greediness is such a trait. To get the ball more than your share of the time, you must be hungry for possession and take it for granted that it should be yours alone.

Nastiness is helpful on the boards, too. You must show the opposing players that it is a painful mistake to get too close to you when you're in search of a rebound. To bother you after you *have* one—well, that would be flirting with disaster!

Impatience is good for rebounding. The pro doesn't stand around gazing upward wistfully. He goes up hard and grabs that orange pumpkin right out of the air, and none too gently, either.

Then there is *noisiness*. Listen to a good rebounder at work! He'll grunt, growl, slam his feet onto the floor as he lands, and in general make a rooting boar sound downright gentlemanly.

All this should give you a picture of the ideal rebounder. He's a rough, mean, ornery customer. He's vital to a fast break (you'll never see a team fast break until after it has the ball back!). He turns missed shots into scores on the offensive boards. He prevents those second and third lame duck or cripple shots (I call them *gifts*—the kind of gifts I don't want my team giving) from the foe.

Here's an interesting statistic: no less than *70%* of the time, the team with the most rebounds wins the game. In other words, rebound or lose.

Your coach will have his own preference as to how you should handle the opponent while you are rebounding. Some believe a strong rebounder should just go get the ball. More often, a coach wants his players to box out the nearest opponent and keep him boxed out. The theory behind this is that, even if the ball drops in front of you while you are maintaining your contact with that other player, you're still going to get it, since you're between the opponent and the ball. Besides, the argument goes, the most common error of players with otherwise good position for a rebound is to rush in too far underneath, allowing the ball to get behind, where the opponent can pick it off.

My preferred rebounding method, and probably the most popular of the various ways, at least at the higher levels, is to get some contact and then go for the ball. My philosophy is that a player who is boxed out even for a second has already been placed at an insurmountable disadvantage. The player who boxes out but then releases to go in for the ball will rarely get too deep, for there just isn't time to go too far in after making sure of getting contact first. The players who don't make any contact whatsoever are the ones we see too far underneath. Besides, failure to move forward after the initial contact may sometimes allow someone other than the player's own man to dash in for the ball, having been improperly defensed.

Whatever method you decide on, it will pay you to know certain principles of rebounding. A rebound comes off on the opposite side from the shooter 75% of the time. Knowing this, you should have some idea of where to go for early position. If you do not have two other rebounders to help you form the ideal rebound triangle in the lane, forget the middle; only 10% of missed shots come into the

When properly positioned for a rebound, a player finds height is irrelevant.

Having taken the rebound, the offensive player keeps the ball up but in front of her and gives the defensive player a shove with the rump.

middle. Box out the person on the weak side if you are alone on the boards.

Since few high school teams make half their shots from outside the lane, you must always expect a shot to be missed. Even in the lane, more than a third of the shots are missed by most teams. Be ready!

Here's a valuable tip: when you are an offensive rebounder and a defensive person is between you and the basket, your best opportunity for securing a rebound will always come when you move *hard toward the baseline*. By the time you fight into the lane on the high side, the rebound will be in someone else's hands. Go to the baseline and then in, every time.

Another important principle: you need to take up space underneath the basket. That means you get the elbows out, seat pushed back, knees flexed. Don't be a harmless cornstalk!

If the ball comes your way, grab it with *two hands*. Some experts suggest that you yank the ball downward, getting one hand on top of it and pulling it down roughly. Just getting both hands on it is more than many do. Too often high school rebounders forget what game they're playing. They think the basketball is a volleyball, to be kept in play by tapping it upward with the fingertips.

Next, land on a *good base*. That means you should come down with feet about shoulder width apart and even, not one forward and one back. If possible, take a half-pivot in midair as you get the ball so you can come down already turned outward for the quick outlet pass. Otherwise you must take the time to pivot after you come down, or worse yet, you will have to throw a pass from a twisting stance instead of being squared up.

You must concentrate on finding an outlet. If you allow contact underneath to bother you, you will waste time and concentration. A speedy outlet is needed for a fast break. It also is your best guarantee against a turnover. If the outlet simply is not there, keep the ball up overhead, particularly if you are tall, or, if you must bring it down, tuck it into your middle and move those elbows. Some like to have a smaller rebounder take the ball all the way down to the knee or ankle area, but that makes it harder to get a pass off quickly.

I far prefer the overhead method. If you maintain a firm grip on that ball, another player will rarely dislodge it or tie you up without being called for a foul. You can also release the ball outside instantly when you spot someone who has freed himself. Especially on the offensive boards, the high position helps, because you can quickly put the ball back up cleanly, whereas after bringing it down you may never get it back up through flailing arms for a decent shot.

Rebounding is fun. It's an adventure. It's an opportunity to develop self-confidence. It brings fast rewards—ball possession, sometimes a score. It gives a determined rebounder a sense of power, accomplishment, and something akin to the feeling of a soldier who emerges from the trenches alive. The art of rebounding has, indeed, been rightly termed *war on the boards*.

chapter thirteen

ways to improve your shooting

Ten thousand shots from now, your shooting will improve. Whether it will increase by 10% or 30%, however, depends on the way you go about practicing. I shudder when I enter a gymnasium in the summertime and see some poor, hopeful soul putting up shots from over the shoulder, while another hard worker is bombing the brave folks under the basket by throwing up shots from the far end. When you practice your shooting, do it correctly. Get in lots of shots, work up a sweat, and go home tired. Take shots you'll find useful later. Shoot correctly. You may find it useful to have a shooting partner. Your partner can help you in several ways:

1. He can check your shooting form by standing under the basket and watching you shoot a couple.
2. He can help motivate you to get to the gym in the first place.

3. He can take turns with you, shooting after a crisp pass (of varying kinds).
4. He can passively or actively defend against your shots to give you practice that duplicates more closely what you will run into during the season.
5. He can take turns rebounding with you so the two of you can get in as many shots, or more, as if you practiced alone.
6. He can force you to go both right and left before shooting.
7. He can provide you with a little competition to make practicing more fun.
8. He may offer you encouragement as you improve.

It is a good idea to start your shooting practices as the player is doing on page 78. By lying on your back and flipping the ball overhead, you force yourself to employ the correct arm position and to maintain proper follow-through.

Start your actual shooting from fairly close in and work out gradually. You are less likely to pick up poor shooting habits this way, and your accuracy will be better as well. For shots in the lane, go hard and keep putting the rebounds back up immediately. Shoot both free throws and lay-ups, shots which many players neglect when on their own.

Once you are a little way out from the basket, if you are working alone, practice the way the player is doing it in the photos on page 79. She faces away from the basket, spins the ball back to herself off a bounce by flipping it outward (backspin); after catching this pass to herself, she executes a good reverse pivot and puts up a quick shot. This is far superior practice to that done by the lazy shooter, who stands facing the basket, takes two or three dribbles, and shoots a set shot; after retrieving the ball, he walks back to the spot he likes and goes through the same routine.

Here are some of the basic things to check for proper form:

- Are you elevating the ball, i.e., shooting from your forehead and not from the chest?
- Is the ball centered so your arms form a triangle (see page 80)?

Begin shooting practice like this to make sure you aren't sliding into bad habits.

Flipping the ball up from this prone position insures that the hand and wrist gooseneck (this means following through) properly; also the correct spin is given to the ball.

As she practices her shooting alone, the player starts the shot facing away from the basket and flipping the ball down with spin, which will bring it back toward her.

The ball comes back, duplicating a pass from another player.

Now she has pivoted to get herself squared up to the basket.

After her pivot her shot is an easy one to make.

The player's arms form a triangle as she prepares to shoot; the ball is just over her forehead or her right eye.

- Are you shooting the ball off the heels of your hand and not burying it in your palms or using just the fingertips? (See the figure on page 81).
- Are you keeping that guide hand underneath and the balance (sideward) hand at the side and not so high that it forces your guide hand to push the ball off it?
- Are you arching the shot enough?
- Are you jumping straight up off a good base and coming down on the same spot?
- Are you following through so that your hand is goosenecked as in the photo on page 82?

The proper shot is illustrated in the photos on page 82.

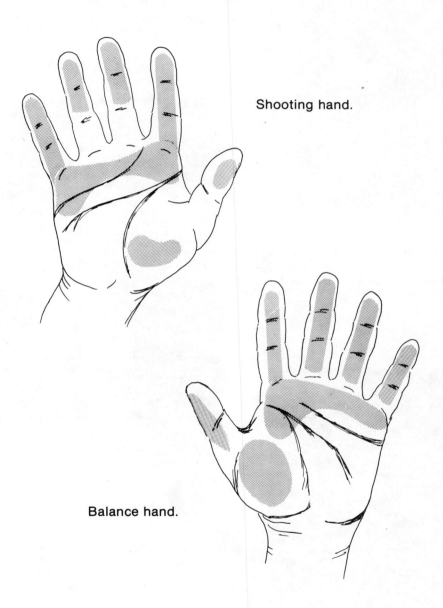

Shooting hand.

Balance hand.

After following through properly, the player's hand is goosenecked, with her fingers pointed forward or downward, not upward.

Do not neglect practicing free throws; take them seriously and concentrate to duplicate the shot you need in a game situation.

You must go straight up on the free throw to allow your legs to give the thrust. Either keep your feet or be sure you come straight back down.

More often than not, failure to attend to one or more of the details outlined above is at the root of a shooting slump. If you discover you are shooting at a basket with a lid on it one of these times, don't panic or quit shooting. The most common shooting problem is lack of arch for girls and lack of follow-through for boys. Girls tend to shoot a flat shot, one right at the basket on a line, while boys tend to release the ball and snap their hands back without gracefully following through the shot with arms stretched outward.

Make certain on the next couple of shots that you aren't failing in either area. If the ball still shies away from the hoop, wait until after halftime to try again (unless you have a lay-up or two; after making an easy shot or two, many slumping shooters are OK once again, so try it and see). Bear in mind that your own fear of missing may be the real key to a slump. The best shooter is barely conscious of his body; after a few misses, he may change his shot slightly due to self-consciousness or tension. If you take a couple hundred shots during the course of the season, you're bound to run into an occasional dry spell, whether you're changing your shot or not. Don't make matters worse by hitting the panic button.

If you think you are especially tired, stretch out slowly and thoroughly during time-outs. A good stretch greatly lessens weariness. Another gimmick that has amazing success is to *smile*. Strange, but true. Smiles relax you. They can even alter a negative mood.

If you are sweaty, wipe your hands off on the driest part of your uniform—your socks. I prefer the knee socks to ankle socks for my ballplayers because they need that dry area for their hands, especially before shooting free throws.

Do not try shots you never practice. Remember to practice shots you will be likely to have in a game. That includes twisting, off-balance shots (70% of all lay-ups are shot off a twist or off balance). It also includes those shots made from four feet to six feet away. Everyone practices the 12- to 15-footers and regular lay-ups. But how many times do players practice the chip shots? In a game, they're worth two points!

chapter fourteen

one on one

A ll basketball boils down to three-, two-, and one-person moves. Of the possible combinations, one-on-one moves are the most basic and constitute the greatest portion of the game. If you are an adept one-on-one player, your chances of excelling in team play are very good as long as you can add to your individual skills the vital quality of unselfishness so that you can adjust to team ball.

When you are playing one on one, try the suggestions in this chapter. The miscellaneous moves and gimmicks suggested here will enhance your play. As you become increasingly successful by adding these important little details to your style of play, you will gain confidence and be better yet.

First of all, master the basic offensive moves that free you to go around the opponent. The most useful is probably the simple change of direction, which consists of sharply pushing the ball on the dribble from the dribble hand to the opposite side and hand. Since this is done in front of the body, it has to be both quick and low. A high bounce leaves dead time during which you are not sufficiently in control of the ball so that it may be slapped free.

The second basic move is a hesitation and hit as shown on page 86. This is a sudden change in forward speed, which leads the defender to expect a directional change, and then a continuation in the same direction at renewed speed to blast past the hesitating defender.

Third is the between-the-legs dribble. This protects the ball better than a simple change of direction. For a moment, the defender may even lose sight of the ball and become confused about where you are headed.

Fourth is the behind-the-back dribble. Once branded a hotdog move, it has become standard in high school and college as well as for pros. If you watch a good female guard even on a high school B team, you can expect to see this dribble executed. It is a change of direction done by passing the dribble around to the opposite hand behind the back. To do this you must come close to carrying the dribble, maintaining the touch control for as long as possible. Be sure to have the receiving hand down and in a ready position to accept the ball as it bounds up on the other side.

Before the dribble is used, you may employ a jab or rocker step to throw the defender off. This consists of a step into the defender while maintaining balance, holding the body fairly upright, so that you can quickly rock back again and make another move. When you execute this step the defender may take a retreat step; if so, his balance will probably be to the rear and you can quickly step back again and shoot. If the defender moves to the right or left, depending on the direction of your jab step, you may then lock his feet (as illustrated in Chapter 5) by taking a step to his side and then drive around. If the defender moves up on you, driving around him is still easier.

When you dribble forward and then stop, execute the Spears pullback dribble. This is a fancy name for a simple maneuver. It just means that, instead of continuing to bounce the ball toward the front, as you stop you pull that last bounce backward to set the dribble down closer to you in a protected position. If you don't do this, the defender may gain possession very easily.

Here the dribbler abruptly stopped her forward motion and straightened slightly as if she were planning to stop dribbling.

Instead of stopping, she suddenly dribbles forward again, past the defensive player (called the *hesitation-and-hit dribble*).

The dribbler is properly protecting the dribble but cannot continue going straight ahead.

The player quickly flips the ball between his legs; the release hand is on the side of the rearward foot, and the receiving hand is the one on the side of the forward foot.

The receiving hand has been down and ready to take the ball so the between-the-legs dribble can be completed quickly and surely; the dribbler will now go hard in the direction of the dribble.

The dribbler must change directions quickly.

The player goes behind her back with the dribble, her receiving hand ready to accept the ball.

She now goes in the direction of the behind-the-back dribble.

Another good move is the fake reverse and continuation. In this move you dribble toward the basket, then maintain the dribble as you plant a foot and start to spin back, apparently to go around the other way. Instead of completing a full turn, you swiftly resume your original path.

If you wish, you can complete the reverse spin and go to the opposite side of the defense. The key to doing this is to be certain you're right up on the defender before spinning off. This move is called by many names; I call it the *spin-off*; some label it a *dribbling reverse, hook,* or *turnaround dribble.*

Any decent ballplayer can throw a good fake. The basic ingredient of a fake is to make it emphatic enough to convince the defender you mean to move that way; then go in the opposite direction without any hesitation whatever so you don't allow the defender the recovery time required to stay with you.

The defender also has some tricks at his disposal. None of them will help unless he is determined to play good defense. Lack of defensive desire dooms anyone to a third-rate performance.

Defense is not played primarily with the hands and arms, but with the *feet.* Move them and keep on moving them! If you get beat, recover and go after the opponent even if it doesn't seem possible to catch him. You may surprise yourself—and him. If you slap at the dribble, slap upward so that you're less likely to be called for a foul. If you keep your palms turned upward, you'll remember this.

Some coaches want you to watch the player's middle, on the assumption that, where the middle goes, he will go. This is unnatural, and I teach my players to follow their instincts and watch the ball. That's what we're after, and where the player goes is important only because he's taking that ball with him!

When you are defensing that ball handler, make yourself wider. The illustrations of this show the difference between a player with elbows out and one with elbows close to the body. Your feet also must be about shoulder width apart between glide steps. (I call the defensive move *gliding,* not *sliding* or *shuffling*, because I want it to conjure up an image of silky smoothness, not bumbling along. The sliding steps are made without crossing the feet or even touching them. Use swift little six-inch foot movements.)

Here the dribbler wants to go by on the defender's left side, but the defender is anticipating her move.

To increase the room in which to get by, the dribbler reverses her direction, bringing the defender upright or in the direction toward which the reversal is made.

Instead of completing the spin-off or reversal, the dribbler comes back around in her original direction and goes past.

Even though the defender has been caught out of position, she can recover if she is willing to move her feet and not give up. The dribbler is on the high side, so with a quick slide the defender may be able to keep her from an easy shot.

The defensive player is straight up and down and will be easy to drive around.

This defensive player is lower and has her elbows outward; she is much harder to get past.

When you are caught out of position or when you are going after a loose ball or rebound, *be an elephant*! Make a racket; let the defender know he's got company; take up all the room you can.

There are ways to psyche out the opponent. Learn some of them. The best way is to talk to him. Don't be nasty or abusive—that's poor sportsmanship. Anything you say will help your psyche-out job as long as it distracts the other player or makes him think about movements his muscle memory should be taking care of. For example, if he makes a good shot, and then you say, "Wow! You really arched that one!" he is going to be thinking about arching the shot on his next attempt and may change his shot just enough to throw it off. If he has a jammed finger or a floor burn, be sympathetic: "Are you okay? That finger still hurting?" It makes him think of his discomfort when he should be oblivious to it. Inviting a shot sometimes wrecks it for him; it implies that you're confident he'll miss. Step back and say, "That's a free one!" when he's 20 feet out. Talking about one of his teammates—"If the guy would pass to you once in a while, you'd have 20 points already!"—may upset him. If you're going for a loose ball and you yell, "I've got it," you can sometimes convince him and he'll let up. Or you can say distracting things that are totally irrelevant to the game—serious or strange or humorous things—to disrupt concentration. I've heard a player holler, "Spaghetti!" to a shooter and make him miss. Ask him how his grades are, or if his dog is going to have pups, or if he enjoys swimming. Conversely, if you maintain a steady conversational banter, you can throw your opponent off by suddenly falling stony silent. Shouting just as he is shooting can unnerve him. Telling him he really concentrates well and doesn't seem to let anything distract him sets him up to become aware of every possible distraction. Of course, you should exercise good judgment and sportsmanship. Be quiet when an opponent is shooting a free throw. Limit your chattering to remarks that are nice, not condescending.

These things won't work every time or with every player. When they do work they're worth it. One danger is that you may be on the receiving end of some return banter. Have a workout companion subject you to these things in practice sessions so you become immune to them.

You can't outplay your opponent one on one if he's in better shape than you are. Do whatever you have to do to pare off excess weight and to toughen up. Otherwise, that fourth quarter can get long. Defense especially requires explosive release of energy.

If you're a sure ball handler, it will be easy to outmaneuver most defensive players. Read the next chapter for drills that will improve your skill. Also learn the shots and moves described in Chapter 17.

One last factor: *confidence*. Without it, you'll feel and look incompetent. With it, you may perform beyond your actual ability. Think highly of yourself. Never be negative. Constantly picture yourself as succeeding. Enjoy yourself as you play; don't get shaken up or upset by anything. You're too big a person to let a bad call or an unkind comment put you into a tailspin. Mistakes shouldn't bother you, either—they're steppingstones to improved play.

chapter fifteen

become a ball handler

At the risk of sounding like a broken record, I must state that repetition is paramount in learning basketball skills. As with so many other basketball skills, becoming a proficient ball handler is dependent on *doing it*, on your own, over and over, until the skill is part of your repertoire. This chapter will give you a list of ball-handling exercises you can use to speed your development.

One gimmick you should not overlook is that you can expand your ball-handling abilities through use of time that most people don't think of using: have a ball in your hands all the time, whether you are riding your bike or sitting in front of the television set. You can carry your basketball with you when you're going to school and on the way home again. You can pick it up and fool around with it while talking on the telephone or in person to friends. Some players have even slept with a basketball at their side. The idea of all this is that you must get the habit of having the ball around and of picking it up whenever you can. It galls me when a player tries to excuse his neglect of ball-handling practice by telling me he was away on vacation, at church camp, etc. Is there a rule against having a basketball along with you when you visit Aunt Minerva in Spokane? Isn't there room enough for a basketball in the family station wagon when you leave for church camp? Don't kid yourself. If you want to handle the ball, you most certainly can and will.

You must develop the skills covered in the preceding chapter if you are to excel at the guard position. Those skills will also make you a better power forward, and even a center is best advised to learn them in order to prepare for a possible role change on the college level. Remember, at 6'8", Magic Johnson plays guard in the pros! You're never too tall to handle the ball.

BALL-HANDLING DRILLS

Here is a list of basic ball-handling drills. Don't confine yourself to these; it's fun to dream up and try new tricks with a basketball. Use your imagination. All the exercises listed here are the result of someone's being inventive. Your brainchild may be a standard drill someday.

Ball Squeeze

Squeeze the ball as hard as you can. This strengthens your fingers and improves your grip. You can set the ball down and squeeze it with one hand, trying to palm it, and you can pick it up and squeeze with both hands.

Squirt

Use your fingertips and squirt the ball out of your hand by increasing the pressure so it pops back and forth from hand to hand without being tossed.

Crunchers

Toss the ball up and catch it with a mean, forceful clap of the palms. Try to pop it like a balloon.

Circles

Pass the ball around your head, neck, waist, each leg, both legs together, ankles. Then reverse the direction. You can get fancier by doing a figure eight through the legs, and fancier still by doing a figure eight and then around over the back and down again.

Figure Eight Roll

Quickly roll the ball with your fingertips around the floor between your feet in a figure eight pattern.

Figure Eight Dribble

Dribble the ball between your legs in a figure eight pattern, keeping it as low as you can. Make sure you go in both directions. Try to reach the point at which you can do it without peeking.

Circle Dribbling

This is the same as circles, but this time dribble the ball around one leg at a time in a circle and then around your legs with the feet together.

Rear Bounce

Known by many names, such as *butt bruiser, duster,* and the *bridge bounce*, this consists of taking the ball out in front of you with two hands, then sharply bouncing it backward so it hits the floor hard between your legs and angles up sharply behind you, where you catch it. Then you can reverse the bounce and catch it again in front.

Overhead Drop

Also commonly known as a back toss, for this exercise, drop the ball backward over your head and quickly drop your arms down and around behind to catch the ball as it drops to your lower back.

Spider Dribble

Dribble the ball between your feet, first one dribble with each hand in front of you, then a dribble with each hand reaching through from behind your legs. Continue this, front and back, rapidly.

Seated Dribble

Sit down and dribble the ball at your side, then at the other side, then back and forth between your legs at the knee as you keep your heels on the floor and your knees up. You can also dribble the ball continuously all the way around you.

Prone Dribble

Lie completely flat on your back and dribble the ball. As you improve at this, try working the dribble around on each side in a pattern. Lie back down, then dribble while lying on your belly.

Spin the Ball

Spin the ball on one finger. You can learn to keep it going with quick finger brushes in the direction of the spin. Then keep it going as you bounce it off a knee, forearm, fist, and head, again catching it on the finger each time. If you have trouble getting started with this, spin it on two fingers together at first, or even on three bunched together. Later you can pass it across your fingertips, one at a time. I've seen a couple of players who could do this together, each spinning a basketball, then flipping it up to the other player and catching his.

Catches

Place the ball behind your neck against your shoulder blades. Release it, clap your hands in front of you, and reach back to catch the ball at your lower back level before it can fall to the floor. Then try progressively lower drop positions until you can hold and release the ball from lower than the knees and still catch it before it hits the floor.

Kneel Dribble

Kneel on one knee with the other up and dribble the ball around and under the knee that is in the air.

The kneel dribble.

Toss and Clap

Toss the ball up high and see how many times you can clap your hands before catching it again.

Behind-the-Back Catch

Toss the ball up and allow it to just miss the back of your head so you can catch it behind you. Toss it a little higher as you catch onto this until you can go up to the rafters with it.

Two-Ball Dribble

Practice dribbling two balls at once, first keeping them going in unison, then staggering the dribble so one hits the floor and then the other. Do this standing, then walking, then running, then backward.

Juggling

Try juggling three balls at once.

The player juggles three basketballs.

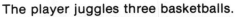

Walking Figure Eight

Pass the ball around your legs in a figure eight while walking forward, first slowly and then faster until you can do it while jogging. Next try moving backward while doing this.

Wall Dribble

Dribble the ball on the wall as rapidly as possible, with no more than a three-inch bounce off the wall each time. First stand and do this, then walk along the wall, keeping the ball going.

Dead-Start Dribble

Place a ball on the floor and start it bouncing with a quick slap from the back of your hand, fingers together and outstretched. As it bounces upward slightly, quickly turn your hand over and maintain the dribble with normal finger positioning.

Body Rolls

Hold the ball out away from you in one palm. Tilt your arm to start it rolling slowly downward along your arm. Tip your head forward and allow the ball to continue rolling across your shoulders and down your other arm. Catch it in the opposite hand from the one you started with.

Knee Dribbling

Keep a dribble going without using your hands by bringing your knees up high and nudging the ball back down with a knee or shin, alternating as you run forward (see photo on page 101.) It's not easy!

Knee dribbling.

Trick Lay-ups

Try doing lay-ups after passing the ball behind and around your waist without setting it down again or traveling; through your legs, up and in; off a 360-degree midair spin; etc.

chapter sixteen

foul trouble

There are three types of fouls: *stupid, lazy,* and *good*. Stupid fouls include these:

- Ones you make against an opponent at his far end of the court, when he can't score anyway.
- Over-the-back fouls when you are obviously out of position to contest a rebound.
- Reaching-in fouls against a player you are guarding and who is keeping the ball protected.
- Technical fouls for questioning referee judgment, using abusive language, or displaying temper.
- Body fouls created by running alongside a dribbler and pushing in on him.

You never need to be guilty of any of these fouls! It's a matter of making up your mind to do your job on the court correctly. Don't take a notion to go after the ball in any of the ways just mentioned. They only cause trouble for you and headaches for your coach.

Remember, there are times when a ball is rightfully the property of your opponent. At such times you have no business going after it. Just guard him! These times include when a rebound comes to him, whether because you are out of position or because the ball simply bounced right to him; when a player properly keeps the ball on his protected side; and when a player tucks the ball into his midsection with his elbows out. It's all right in these situations to let that player maintain control of the ball. Your assignment is to stay in proper position and wait for him to make a mistake; *then* take the ball away.

A lazy foul is one you commit because you're not working hard enough to be where you should be. When you aren't guarding the baseline properly and your man scoots by you, your laziness defensively may lead you to this type of foul—you stick out a knee, throw an arm in front of him, or give him a bump from the side. Move your feet so he can't start that drive around you to begin with. Don't be lazy.

A good foul is one you commit accidentally due to playing hard. When you go all out during a game, you're going to make contact with other players, and on occasion that's going to mean you'll be called for a foul. Don't let it bother you. In fact, if you never foul, *that* should worry you more. It means you're not aggressive enough or you're hanging back when you should be going for the ball.

Another type of good foul, or so some coaches teach, is the one you get stopping a sure lay-up. Making the opponent earn his two points by making two 15-foot shots instead of getting the two from a lay-up makes good sense in some cases. Some coaches, including many very good coaches, strongly disagree. Their philosophy is that (1) that sure lay-up isn't always so sure and (2) getting a foul leads to the one-and-one situation against your team that much quicker and also to your being in foul trouble and on the bench. Whichever way your coach teaches, know his policy and stick to it.

There are some little things you can do to avoid some fouls. For instance, when you set a screen, put your hands on your knees or just above them (a few coaches suggest placing the palms against the side of your leg). This eliminates the temptation to stick that knee out as the other player goes around.

Another trick is to learn the proper use of elbows (see photos below). Don't swing your elbows—that's just as bad as tucking them in. Pivot sharply with the elbows held outward, locked in place.

When you are guarding a dribbler and think you can knock the ball loose, do so with an upward slap, not by batting downward. When you swing your arm downward you are more likely to hit the dribbler's arm, and you are more visible to the referee. To make sure you're swinging upward only, keep your palms turned upward while playing defense on the man with the ball.

If you are trying to stop a man who has broken up court ahead of the pack for what appears to be an uncontested lay-up, do two

The player takes the rebound with good body positioning: her feet are apart, giving her a solid base, and she is taking up space with her elbows and rump.

As she turns, she can keep the defender away with her elbows. This is legal because she is turning with the shoulders, not swinging her elbows only.

This is an offensive foul. The offensive player should
not swing her elbows only.

As the dribbler picks up the dribble to start his lay-up,
the defensive player can hit the ball away by tapping
upward.

things: make a racket, so he's worried about what may befall him as
he tries his shot, and try to time it so you can slap the ball loose at the
instant when he picks up his dribble. That's the only time you can
safely hit the ball. Any other time you are risking hitting an arm (or
at least a hand, which will usually be called a foul even though
technically the hand is part of the ball and can be hit without
fouling).

If you are setting a pick and someone runs into you, don't try to
keep your balance. Keep your feet right where they are and take the
fall. This makes it plain to the referee that you established position
before you were contacted. You can use your hands to break your
fall, but not until the last second.

An offensive player sets a blind pick on the defender.

The dribbler must drive the defender directly into the pick before changing direction to go around.

The player setting the pick must keep her feet still as long as possible and allow herself to fall backward without moving her feet from their original position.

Because the dribbler did not drive the defender straight back, and because the pick setter did not keep her hands on her thighs or hips, a foul is committed with the knee.

A final tip: having your hands on the ball helps prevent many foul calls. If you hang back for a fraction of a second before a collision so that the other man gets the ball, that collision probably will be judged to be your fault. If the ball is up for grabs, take it without hesitation.

Go straight up like this to block and do not swing the arm to bat the ball away.

chapter seventeen

big league moves

Pro ballplayers do all the things high school players do. They just do them better. A reverse slam dunk won't make you a pro-style shooter if you can't make a free throw or a regular forward lay-up. Practice the tough shots and the trick shots, and learn the shots pictured in this chapter, but don't neglect for even one day working on the basic bread-and-butter shots every player needs.

Some of these shots may be considered grandstand moves. But what's wrong with a little of that? If you're good, it's nice to know it and fun to show it. I think a little flair in one's playing style adds to that all-important characteristic of a fine player: *confidence*. Just don't go so overboard that you antagonize your fellow players or upset your coach! And don't try a fancy shot in a game until after you've mastered it through hours of practice. It's embarrassing to put on a flashy move and turn the ball over without scoring!

Some of the shots and moves that were considered show-off stuff in the not-too-distant past have become stock-in-trade for college and professional athletes. The behind-the-back dribble is a standard tool in high school games. The behind-the-back pass is a regular offensive weapon in college ball. As the sport continues to produce more able athletes, brand-new shots and moves will be invented, and some of them will become widespread.

You can develop a behind-the-back pass quite quickly. Mark a spot on the wall. Hit it by passing the ball behind your back. Then hit it again while walking parallel to it. Next increase your speed. Before long you can rifle an on-target behind-the-back pass while going full speed, and then you can learn to do it with hardly even a turn of the head toward the target. (See photos on page 110).

Before you try passing the ball behind your back, you must be able to handle a lookaway pass. All this means is that you can pass the ball without eyeing your receiver. It's simple but deceptive. It demands good peripheral vision. This is one basketball skill you can practice in a classroom. As you use your side, or peripheral, vision, it will improve. Actually, the vision itself isn't improving, but you learn to recognize its existence and to trust it. (See page 111).

A turnaround jump shot is hard to defend. Get one. Start with a half-twist in the air, then work farther around until you can be accurate even with a complete twist that is begun with your back to the basket. (See photos on page 112.)

At one time a fallaway jumper (called a *fadeaway shot* in the 1950s) was thought to be a neat move. But it fell into disrepute as coaches stressed elevating the shot and employing arch to avoid blocks. Now, the shot is once again being recognized as a legitimate one. It consists of jumping both upward and away from the defender, instead of straight up as in a normal shot. At the peak of the jump, you will be a foot or two farther back from where you started the jump. This shot is difficult to execute. The tendency is to let the shot fall short of the rim. Since it will be released from a point behind where you line it up, it is important that you remember to add a few inches to the depth of the shot to compensate.

The common hook shot was once uncommon. High school forwards who tried it were chastised. Some centers could get by with it

A behind-the-back pass.

If the pass has confused the defensive player, the passer may be able to get around for a return pass (give-and-go play).

The lookaway pass: the passer spots a
wide-open teammate out of the corner
of his eye (uses peripheral vision).

Continuing to look away from the direction in which he is going with the
ball, the offensive player fires the pass.

An over-the-shoulder check tells the player that the defensive man is directly behind him and will be hard to get around.

The player spins as he jumps upward.

The shot is off and his follow-through may enable him to draw a foul on the defender as well.

The player takes a check over her shoulder.

She executes a turnaround jump shot, falling away as she does so instead of lunging forward at the basket. If she had gone forward or even straight up, the taller defender might have been able to block the shot, but her fadeaway shot has plenty of room.

The offensive player receives the ball in the middle
of the lane with a defensive player behind her.

She executes a pivot to face the basket and can see
that a regular shot against the taller defender might
be blocked.

Reaching out and around, she flips
the ball up from outside the
defensive player's reach, giving the
shot plenty of clearance.

if they were in close. Now even a guard ought to master it. It's another of those hard-to-block shots. Kareem Abdul-Jabbar has made the hook sacred with his awesome "sky hook." His shot, of course, has a much different trajectory than yours will, unless you're also 7'2" plus. Learn to shoot a "soft" hook, allowing the ball a chance to roll around and drop through. It's the same principle as the underhanded free throw, which was once considered a better percentage shot than overhand free throws because of the deadened effect of that sort of release. A hook also must be a marshmallow, or pumpkin, when it drops onto the rim area. Otherwise it is a low-percentage shot, a good bet to bound out off the rim or bangboard.

Easier than a hook, but first cousin to it and almost as useful, is the half-hook reacharound shot illustrated in the photos. It gets you around the defender so the shot won't be blocked, then compensates for the increased angle. The shot is different from a normal hook shot. You must get as much of your upper body beyond the defender as possible. (In the normal hook shot you are practically straight up and down, relying on the arc of the ball to keep it from the defender.) The arm is extended *outward* as well as upward, which helps to get the ball past the defender. Thus, the ball is released from a point much lower than in a normal hook shot. Extra wrist action is required because the ball has a farther distance to travel to get to the basket because of the lower release point.

A crossunder, or reverse, lay-up, is illustrated in the photos on page 116. It is often possible to shoot a lay-up on the opposite side from which you drive, as you may be more open after continuing through underneath the basket. If you practice the shot, you may be able to perform it turning either way and with either hand. It's harder to see the basket the way the shot is put up (pages 116–17), but the shot works if you get comfortable with it first in practice.

The shots most loved by basketball fans are the dunks. There are many kinds. The basic dunk shot is the one-handed or two-handed dunk smashed into the net from the same side as the approach. A reverse dunk whether one- or two-handed, is made after crossing underneath. If the angle is toward the bankboard and you have enough height and spring to make such a shot, you must be very careful not to hit your head on the bankboard.

The player steps into the lane with the ball.

She keeps her eyes on the basket as she comes around, and her step will take her to the side of the basket opposite where she started.

She goes up for a left-handed lay-up after crossing underneath.

In this instance, the offensive player is able to go in front of the defender but feels she is too crowded to get off a regular lay-up.

She crosses underneath again and executes a tough shot from the opposite side. Having practiced the shot, she can count on a good percentage with it because it allows enough room over the defensive player's reach.

A conventional dunk, one-handed.

A harder dunk shot, two-handed and reaching under to release at the far side of the rim.

Hanging on the rim is, of course, illegal. It is also dangerous *not* to! When you are first learning to dunk and you don't grab that rim long enough to regain your balance, you run a high risk of spraining an ankle or twisting a knee. Of course, grabbing the rim has its dangers, too—many dunkers get torn fingers from catching a rough edge atop the rim. Usually referees will allow just a moment's hang time on the rim. They know the shot is far harder to complete than it seems it would be. Just don't stay up there too long in a game.

The dunk shot is demoralizing to an opponent and electrifying to one's own side. Nothing can generate the adrenalin needed to start a rally more quickly than a good dunk. If you are close to being able to dunk the ball, it's worth your while to learn the shot. Start with a tennis ball, then go to a volleyball, then try a junior high basketball, then use a regular basketball. If you can reach the rim but need a couple more inches of spring to dunk, work on those leg muscles until you can manage the shot (see Chapter 11).

Tip-in shots are noticeable and impressive. The only way to make them is to throw the ball against the board a few thousand times in practice and tip it in. The advantage of the tip-in, obviously, is that no one has a chance to rebound the ball or to stop your shot if you rebound it.

Pro players are not allowed to use zones. They sometimes do, of course, and are called for a technical foul if they're caught. It isn't easy to detect a zone until the offense shifts radically, since a man-to-man defense may allow for sagging into the lane when away from the ball. However, pros do use man-to-man principles most of the time. Watch them. They are marvelous executors of the defense. One of the basic principles of good man-to-man play is fighting through screens. Pros must do this well. If they fail and a switch with a teammate is needed, the extreme variation in the height of pro players leads to mismatches, and the offense has too big an edge. Pros have to hang with the men they're guarding if at all possible.

In high school some coaches teach players to switch when a screen or pick is used. If your coach tells you to do so, you should, or defensive mayhem will result. If he tells you to fight through the screen, do so as shown in the photos. If a screen is set, watch out for the roll off it. (Pages 122–123 show the screen-and-roll.)

Additional moves you must learn to be truly qualified in your sport include the between-the-legs dribble (See Chapter 14), hesitation lay-ups, underhand lay-ups, and shots from the lane with your left hand (or right, if you're left-handed). Everyone learns to shoot a left-handed lay-up, but a good player also shoots a left-handed jumper when in close and guarded on the right side.

The offensive duo attempts to set up a screen play.

The defensive player who has been guarding the screener "shows," i.e., steps out far enough to let the dribbler know he can cover him, but not too far, so he can still jump back to cover his own man.

The other defender is able to "fight through," getting a leg behind the screener's heel and hooking his upper arm with an elbow as he throws his shoulders back.

Both offensive players are still covered by the original defender.

Again, the screen is set.

This time the defensive player covering the ball loses balance and cannot fight through.

The defenders are forced to switch, but the screened player is behind his man and his teammate's man.

This enables the screener to step away for a pass from the dribbler (called a *screen and roll*).

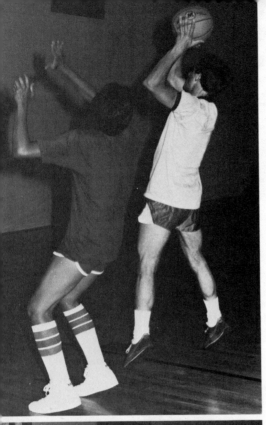

The player goes up for a lay-up and uses "hang time," a hesitation at the peak of the jump before releasing the shot.

Now the defender has declared himself, and the shooter is able to finish the shot without being blocked.

Notice that his hand position has changed: he has not released a regular lay-up from the original hand position but has brought the ball around to release it underhanded. As he does this the defender's blocking hand is past the ball, leaving it in the clear as well as increasing the odds for a three-point play if the defender swings his arm.

The shooter goes up for a lay-up with the defender right with him.

All the defender's arm swing can do now that the ball is gone is to slap the shooter's arm and give him a free throw.

chapter eighteen

when you mean business

Is basketball your number one sport? Do you intend to become as good at it as you can or are you after something for nothing? If you are a sincerely committed player, ready to pay whatever price required for excellence, this chapter is exclusively for you.

You must practice *longer* than anyone else. You must practice *harder* than others do, going all out whether you're alone, playing one on one, playing in a scrimmage, doing team drills, or playing in a game. Watch to see what others are doing; then do more.

We've talked about getting those precious edges that add up to make you a little better than the next guy. One of those edges consists of *what* you practice, as well as how or how long you work. For example, everyone shoots some lay-ups, but when you mean business you'll keep in mind that 70% of all lay-ups in a game are shot off balance or out of position, so you'll practice shooting such shots. A lay-up situation that arises frequently in a game and for which most players are unprepared in practice is shown in the photos.

The shooter is too far underneath to get off an easy lay-up, but he is committed and must try it.

Despite his poor position, the shot is successful, because of previous hours of practice on difficult, twisting shots.

Change-of-direction shots aren't seen much in practice sessions, but they are needed in games. In your practices, work hard on going one way, then getting a shot off in the direction opposite to your movement. Learn to go to your right and left before stopping to release your shot.

Work out faithfully on weights. You don't need a sophisticated program. Just find the maximum weight you can handle, then reduce it to just over half and perform your repetitions. All basketball players need leg strength, and for rebounding upper body strength is even more important, so work on that, too. If you have no set of weights and can't get into a school gym, find something at home you can lift. Whenever you've worked on weights, stretch out thoroughly, or you can nullify the gain in strength by losing quickness and agility.

Many coaches stress the value of "floor sense," but almost no one *practices* it. Floor sense just means knowing where you are at all times on the court, without having to check your feet. It helps you avoid stepping out of bounds, getting out of position on shot attempts, starting a play from too far out, setting screens in awkward places, being in the wrong place for rebounds, etc. To develop it, mark some spots on your home court or find some places on the gym court you can practice going to and shooting from. Start by going to one spot repeatedly until you can do it without looking, regardless of where you start. Then add other spots until you find you always know exactly where you are.

Sincere players face the dilemma of either giving up another sport that might be fun and helpful to development or giving up extra practice time in basketball. Here's how to analyze the problem: first determine honestly how many hours of basketball practicing you think you will get in every day if you don't go out for that other sport. Don't be unrealistic about it. You can burn yourself out if you're locked into practicing more than you really want to, but the fear of burning out needn't bother you if you really want to practice for as long as you set for yourself. A lot of the business of burning out is myth. People who burn out are people who feel forced to spend time on the game and do so without really wanting to; they're not strongly self-motivated for the sport. In fact, a positive addiction is built up by athletes who work out faithfully, whether they're basketball players, joggers, or whatever. After the first month of practicing you'll hit a plateau which, when surpassed, leads to psychological addiction to what you're doing so that you feel almost deprived when you can't practice.

If you have decided on anything fewer than three hours of daily practice, it's worth it to you to participate in other sports. If you're going to practice hard for five hours a day, you can get by without worrying about athletics other than basketball. Few players will want to practice even three hours daily, so in almost all cases you should go out for as many other sports as you can. The physical skills developed will help you play better basketball, and it will be a good change of pace.

Volleyball, football, tennis, racquetball, handball, soccer, wrestling, softball, baseball, and swimming, to name some of the commonly offered sports, can all benefit you as a basketball player if the season doesn't conflict with basketball season. Don't sit in study hall or spend your time watching television if you have an opportunity to go out for these activities.

Track isn't optional for basketball players. It's a necessity. There is no substitute for it. It is the best conditioning sport you can find. It will help you develop guts, determination, stamina, self-discipline, a winning attitude, speed, quickness, strength, self-respect, confidence, and pride in yourself.

Track is healthful. It will prolong your life. It will tone you up and make you feel better all over, all the time. You will become more resistant to colds and other ailments. You'll have fewer ankle problems. If you have the opportunity to go out for track but use some flimsy excuse for not doing so, you will live to regret it. No one ever says later, "I wish I hadn't worked so hard," or "I wish I hadn't sacrificed so much for basketball." Many do say, "I wish I had put more into it," or "I wish I'd made an honest effort," or "I wish I'd given it a try." *So do it.* If you're too lazy, you'll stay that way or get worse. Lazy people are poor athletes and don't usually amount to much in any other area, either. They just glide along, barely getting by, making their excuses and complaining when things don't come to them the easy way.

You can't always have your cake and eat it, too. There are some extracurricular activities that take up your time without helping your basketball skills. Take a cold, hard look at your schedule. If you choose to excel in basketball instead of being mediocre in several activities, you may find it best to drop some nonessentials.

I am not advocating being a lopsided person. You can find some activities outside athletics that are not demanding or don't require as much of your time. If you get into everything, you may be so tired and listless after a while that you find you have lost your zest and, with it, the benefits of participation. Also, some activities aren't attractive for legitimate reasons. As an example, do you want to be a cheerleader to improve yourself or to spend time with your friends, to run around, or to be a member of a clique? If you have such motives, dump the activity before it's too late.

Life demands choices of us. Making decisions is something you should be able to do. Make your decisions according to what your true priorities are. If basketball comes right after family and academic achievement, honor it ahead of lesser priorities in your decision making. It's that simple.

chapter nineteen

make practice better

There are two primary ways of making a practice session better for yourself. First, make it tougher; second, make it more fun.

You won't get a tough practice playing against weaker competition. If you can't find someone with ability equal to yours or better, stack the odds against yourself by taking on two or more poorer players or going against three with a partner.

When you are having scrimmages, keep a private tally of your fouls. Try to avoid fouling unnecessarily, the same as you will later in an actual game. Don't let other violations go, either, if they are yours. The "NBA shuffle" is the easiest to fall into—taking that extra little step as you're setting the ball down. If you find you've done so, call it and pay the price of a turnover. You'll break the habit in a hurry. If you don't, your sloppiness will carry over into games. You have your high school and college career to complete before you are allowed the luxury of the NBA shuffle! It's overlooked in the pros because fans want to see action, not turnovers. If you step on a line when bringing the ball in, call it. On the other hand, don't get fussy about calling others' violations. You will get jostled many times in games, and you'll observe other players getting away with things. Learn now not to complain.

Don't put up with slack rules, such as insistence on "free ins." Part of the game of basketball is safely relaying the ball onto the playing area. You should practice doing it. Another lazy rule is "even numbers," the rule that states that no one may score on a fast break unless there are as many defensive as offensive players up court. You'll get your transitions down better and get into better condition if you insist this rule be abolished.

Camps and clinics provide good competition. Get to as many as you can. Plan ahead so you'll have the money to go. You must do so to keep up with what even average players are doing. Check with players who have gone to different camps about which camps are good. If you're confident that you are an above-average player, ask your coach to get you invited to invitational camps where better players go. Don't worry about not being the best one there—you're there to improve. Eventually you may be the best one.

If you absolutely can't find people for a decent scrimmage, handicap yourself by spotting the weaker player(s) some points or giving yourself one point per basket to their two. That way you'll have to work hard to stay ahead and won't pick up lazy habits. You can handicap yourself by shooting only left-handed shots when inside 12 feet or, if you have a partner, you can prescribe a certain number of passes between you before you're allowed to shoot.

It's wise to find yourself a partner for the off-season. It's more fun to work with another person. Get someone who is a decent player and who is dedicated. It's no use having a partner who won't show up. Find one you can jog with and who is willing to work on weights and jump ropes as well as play ball. Share goals with your partner and ask him to check you on your shooting form periodically and to point out any flaws he can spot in your playing.

Never hesitate to teach anyone the game, when you have the opportunity—a younger brother or sister, a neighbor kid you're baby-sitting. Become a coach. By teaching them the fundamentals of basketball, you keep reminding yourself of important aspects of playing. As you illustrate moves and shots, you'll sharpen up your own. They'll appreciate your time and attention, and it will allow you to have a basketball in your hands.

When you are working alone, practice can get long and boring unless you exercise a little imagination. You need to shoot many, many more baskets than you will just scrimmaging, so get in those solo or partner shooting hours. If you're shooting one shot over and over to perfect it, make a game of it. It doesn't matter if someone with less creativity would think your mental games are silly.

Play "Undefeated Season." You shoot the shot you're working on and, if you make three in a row, that's a win. If you miss two in a row, it's a loss. See if you can get through a make-believe basketball season with an unblemished record, and then go into post-season play. If the shot is too hard, make it easier—two in a row for a win, three misses for a loss.

Try keeping your percentage over 50 or 100 shots; then see if you can beat it. Or just pretend you're going up for the buzzer shot in a state championship game, or you're being observed while trying out for an NBA team. How about setting yourself a time limit and seeing if you can make a certain number of baskets in that time? Or you can play the "Fifty Percent" game, scoring two for your side for every one you make and counting two for the other side for misses. Make it as hard or as easy as you like, depending on how many lay-ups you allow yourself, or after a miss give yourself a chance to cancel it with a one-and-one at the free throw line.

You can dream up dozens of other mental contests and games to keep shooting practice interesting. While you're doing it, put in some painless practice on pivots by spinning the ball backward to yourself while facing away from the basket, then pivoting around for the shot. Another way is to bounce the ball off a wall, catch it, pivot, and shoot. When you miss, follow the shot up and make the close one—it duplicates what you ought to do in games.

You can see how many free throws you can make with only three misses or no misses. Know what your record is and try to set a new one. Do a little ball handling between shots. It's satisfying to find you can do something better than you used to.

A reward system can be of benefit. If you reach whatever goal you choose to set during a shooting session, buy yourself a Gatorade. If you don't reach the goal, settle for water. Some other treat may suit you, instead, if it isn't damaging to your system.

You can play "Around the World" by yourself. See how many turns you need to go around or just pretend you're two people and compete with yourself. Start up close with a bank shot by the edge of the lane, then work outward, shooting from designated places. If you miss, you have the option of trying again ("risking it"). If you make the second try, you continue, but if you miss it, you start over.

"Twenty-one" can also be a solo game. You get a shot from the free throw line or the top of the key, whatever you choose. If you make it, you score it as two points and then get a shot from in the lane for an additional point before trying another long one. You can play the "Hotshot" game, too, scoring different amounts, from one to five, depending on the difficulty of the shot, and seeing how many points you can rack up in one minute.

chapter twenty

a positive approach

This is the most important chapter in this book. Your mental outlook can make or break you. It not only determines how much of your potential will be realized in basketball, but how far you will get in life itself. In order to have every edge you can scratch up in the game of basketball, you must tend to the mental as well as the physical side of your game.

Giving up, getting mad, being lazy, feeling cheated, pouting, being jealous, lacking team unity and spirit, feeling hesitant and inferior, getting nervous in the clutch—all these are excuses that steamroll your chances of success into forgotten dreams. Get rid of them! Do it now!

Have you ever looked at the other person's side of things? That "unfair" referee is probably a kindhearted, sincere family man trying to put food on the table by putting up with abuse from fans and coaches. He is probably in love with basketball and wants to be close to the game. He will very likely tell your coach and others during or after the game that he sees real talent in you (if the talent is there). He may know it when he has made a questionable call, but he's stuck with it as much as you are. He has feelings and he is almost certainly honest. It's the frustrated player who is biased and narrow-minded on call after call.

When you're involved in an all-out effort to win a game, do you really think you can be fairer than that referee? If you stop and honestly take a look at what the man is doing, can you say he is trying to cheat you? He isn't. I've never seen a referee deliberately cheat anyone, though many times I've thought so during the heat of battle. The longer I am involved with basketball, the more respect I have for referees. I have never regretted giving a ref the benefit of the doubt, but I know many coaches who have regretted flying off the handle.

A referee is a human being. He wants to do his job well. He may be out of shape and so doesn't always get into the best position to make a call, but he makes the call to the best of his knowledge. Some referees are in better shape than some players, and they work hard to be where they should for every play. Give them some of the credit they deserve. Without them, the game would be a free-for-all. Their being there protects you from serious injury and allows your team to compete at basketball instead of in a brawl. Do you like being second-guessed every time you make a decision? Of course not. Neither does a referee, and he isn't going to be any more in your favor because of those stormy looks and little gasps you utter at each call.

The coach also has a job to do. He can do only so much. He knows what he knows and no more. If you or someone you know knows more, that's very nice, but it's also beside the point. The school hired your coach to coach you. During his practices and in the games he is coaching, you have an obligation to do as he directs. If an army is a unit, it can survive, but if it is a mass of disagreeing individuals, it is a mob. A team is unified only when it listens to and obeys its coach. He may not know everything there is to know about basketball, but neither do you and neither does any other coach. He doesn't have to know everything to be successful, as long as you try to learn from him what he *can* teach.

You should be a loyal person. When you are off the court and away from school, don't ever be guilty of bad-mouthing another player or your coaches. You'll pay by losing your own confidence in them, and your lack of confidence filters through and affects them and their confidence. If you run another player down, that player has the right to treat you the same way. Are you perfect enough to be willing to run that risk? Wouldn't you rather have your teammate's support?

You can't be too harsh with yourself, either. For one thing, we all have good and bad days. Don't excuse poor training or laziness as due to a bad day, but if you're trying hard and nothing goes right, it may be just a down time for you, due possibly to cycles that all people undergo. While girls' cycles are more physically apparent, and have been researched to a greater extent, it is now known that boys have their own version of the cycle, too. It can show itself in tiredness, lack of sharpness, inability to concentrate, etc. It will pass. Put in your time, keep working hard, and let time take care of it.

Decide how you want to impress others. If you don't mind being known as a whiner, a critic, or a thundercloud, go to it. If you would rather be known as a cheerful person, one others like to be around, a happy go-getter, a nice person, then now is the time to become that person. You will become whatever you want to be if you start right now and act that way. Don't fall for fables about redheads having tempers, or being crabby because you were weaned too early, or being stuck with the personality you developed before you were six. *You can be what you want to be*. It's something you can make up your mind to, and do.

Keep in mind that others are different. That's OK. You want variety in your life. If everyone was as devoted to basketball as you are, imagine how hard it would be to excel! Be glad that there are those who consider debating, cheerleading, dating, riding horses, or gymnastics more important than basketball. They can't understand how you can be so nutty about your game. Go easy on them. Don't expect them to be understanding all the time, even if they happen to be dear friends or family members. Your mother's job at the ad agency is important to her, so show you care. You want approval, and so does she. Maybe basketball is more important to you than the latest sportswear campaign, but it isn't more important than your mother. Get your priorities lined up.

Best wishes to you as you give basketball—and life—your best shot. Live so that you will have the fewest regrets possible, but remember that everyone has some. Concentrate on doing the best you can in everything for the most rewarding life.

glossary

Bangboard: The glass, metal, or wood surface above and to the sides of the basket, used for carom shots taken from an angle, particularly lay-ups.

Bank, bank shot: A shot that hits the bangboard first and caroms off it into the basket.

Bankboard: See "Bangboard."

Baseball pass: A long one-handed pass to a receiver up court.

Baseline: The end line of the basketball court, stretching between the sidelines and running under the basket.

Block: (a) To stop a shot by stretching upward so that it strikes the hands or forearms; (b) a foul committed by impeding another player's progress by moving into him; (c) the rectangle along the free throw line marking the rebounding area nearest the basket.

Bounce pass: A pass that strikes the floor just over halfway from the passer to the receiver, then bounds up to the receiver's midsection.

Box: See "Block (c)."

Box and one: A defense in which one player is playing man to man and the other four players are playing zone in the lane area.

Boxing out: Keeping an opposing player behind you so he cannot rebound the ball.

Breaking a press: Defeating the purpose of a press by scoring or at least getting the ball safely up court to set up an offense.

Camp: In this book, the term refers to off-season clinics at which players may board for a week or longer.

Charge: An infraction committed by the player with the ball when he dribbles or leaps into a defensive player who has established proper defensive position.

Chest pass: A two-handed pass delivered with a snap of the wrist from chest level to the receiver's chest level.

Clinic: Used interchangeably with *camp* in this book; a teaching session or sessions for basketball players or coaches.

Combination defense: A defense such as a box and one or triangle and two in which some players are playing zone and one or more others man-to-man.

Cut: (a) To eliminate a player who tries out for a team; (b) to move sharply into the lane from outside it.

Defense: Team play when the other side has the ball and must be prevented from scoring if possible.

Delay, delay game: Slowing the game up by a deliberate offense that does allow lay-ups or sometimes any good percentage shot within from six to 12 feet of the basket (used to alter the tempo against a team that likes to run hard).

Denial, denying: Not permitting the player being guarded to have the ball (accomplished by taking a position at his side and keeping an arm up across his chest level).

Diagram code: The basketball picturing system to show plays, which includes the following symbols:

←————————— movement

← — — — — — a pass

←⌐_⌐_⌐_⌐ a dribble

←• • • • • • a shot

├———————— movement ending with a pick or screen

↰└———————— a screen and roll

O   usually a defensive player

X   usually an offensive player

Dribble: Advance the ball by bouncing it.

Drive, drive in, drive the lane: To dribble the ball into close-range scoring position.

Double-team: To guard one player with two.

Dunk, dunk shot: A shot blasted into the basket with the release coming after it has entered the cylinder.

Fake (feint): To indicate intention to go in one direction without actually doing so.

Fast break: To advance the ball swiftly up court in hope of scoring when more offensive than defensive players are in position.

Field goal: Any score in basketball other than a free throw.

Fight through: To stay with the player being guarded despite his use of a pick or screen, by forcing one's way through between the player and his picker or screener.

Flash cut: A sudden cut into the lane for a possible pass in and easy score; then, if the ball is not passed, jumping back out on the side from which entry was made.

Foul: A violation involving contact with another player (or, in the case of most technical fouls, unsportsmanlike conduct of some kind).

Freelance play: An offense allowing individual choices, as opposed to a set play.

Free throw: An unguarded shot granted due to a foul.

Free throw lane: All the area between the lines running from the ends of the free throw line to the baseline.

Free throw lane extended: An imaginary set of lines outward toward midcourt as an extension of the free throw lane boundaries.

Free throw line: The line from which free throws are shot.

Free throw line extended: An imaginary line extended toward the sideline from the free throw line.

Freeze: To hold the ball without an attempt to score. See "Stall."

Front, fronting: Guarding a player by taking a position between him and the ball.

Go both ways: Use the left and right hand instead of being able to use only one of them.

Hook, hook shot: A shot taken sideways with a looping arm motion over the head.

Hook pass: A pass made with the same motion as a hook shot.

Inbounds pass: The pass onto the playing area from out of bounds.

Inbounds play: A set play (designed play, not freelance) to score when the ball is passed in under one's own basket.

Inside: The area close to the basket, usually the lane, called *inside* because when the ball or man is there, the defense has been penetrated.

Jab step: See "Rocker Step."

Jump, jump ball: Two players from opposing teams attempt to tip the ball to a teammate as it is tossed up for them by an official, usually to start a quarter or because both players grabbed the ball at the same time.

Jumpdump, jumpdump pass, jump pass: A pass released downward from the top of a jump, usually a faked shot attempt.

Jump shot: A shot taken at the peak of a spring into the air.

Key: (a) The area from the baseline to the top of the circle, including the free throw lane and free throw circle, so named because it is shaped like a giant keyhole; (b) to signal a play to be run.

Lane: The area between free throw boundaries and from the end line to the free throw line.

Lay-up: A close-in shot laid up so that its momentum carries it into the basket, usually off the bangboard.

Lob, lob pass: A looping pass over the defense, often a high-risk pass because its flight allows time for the defense to recover and get to it.

Lookaway pass: A pass made using peripheral vision only.

Man to man, man-to-man defense: Defense played by having players assigned to specific opponents regardless of where they go on the court.

Man-to-man offense: Any offense designed for use against a man-to-man defense.

Man-to-man press: Guarding man to man immediately when the other team gets the ball, before it is advanced to the other end.

Matchup zone: A sophisticated zone defense that looks like a man-to-man defense.

Mikan drill: Any of several post-man drills in the underbasket area, usually involving pivots and lay-ups.

Offense: (a) The side with the ball or (b) the pattern followed in an attempt to score.

Off hand: The weaker, usually left, hand.

Outlet: The pass to a player waiting in the clear after a rebound, or that player.

Out-of-bounds play: See "Inbounds play."

Outside: Away from the basket; See "Inside."

Over and back: Crossing the midcourt stripe and returning, a violation.

Overshift: Guarding a ball handler half the width of the body to one side.

Pattern: A play or offense.

Perimeter: An area along the outside of the general area close to the basket.

Period: A quarter of play in high school or pro ball (in college two halves are played without a breakdown into quarters).

Peripheral vision: Side vision ("corner of the eye" vision), seeing without directly looking at what is seen.

Pick: Stationing oneself so that the defensive man guarding the ball handler will be unable to stay with him, having run into the picker.

Pivot: Planting a foot and rotating in a partial spin with the weight on the ball of the planted (pivot) foot.

Play: A prescribed set of movements designed to score.

Point: The spot in the center of the top of the circle.

Point guard: The guard whose duty it is to initiate the offense, usually from a spot on or near the point.

Post, post man: A player who stations himself near the lane.

Press: To guard before the ball has come up court.

Press breaker: A pattern designed to get the ball up court against a press and, hopefully, to score.

Quarter: A period of play.

Quick break: After a turnover, the ball is brought up court on the dribble for an uncontested lay-up.

Rebound: To secure possession of a ball as it comes off the board or rim following a miss.

Release: (a) To stop playing defense and go on offense early, before the rebound, so position farther up court may be gained; (b) to let the ball go on a pass or shot.

Reverse lay-up: A lay-up shot made after crossing underneath the basket to the far side.

Rocker step: A step forward or toward one side while keeping the pivot foot in place, so that a move may be made in another direction after the extended foot is drawn back (also called *jab step*).

Safety: An offensive player who remains farther out than the defense as a shot goes up so that he will have good defensive position following a change of possession.

Scout: To look at and evaluate another team or player; also one who does this.

Screen: Similar to a pick, but away from the ball, used to free a player to receive a pass in the open and in scoring position.

Screen and roll: The movement following a screen in which the screener follows into the lane so he may have scoring position if the pass cannot be made to the player who was first given a screen.

Scrimmage: Gamelike practicing with two sides and scores, but sometimes fewer than five on a side.

Set play: A designed play that is not a shuffle because the players do not end up in the original places from which they started.

Set shot: A shot taken without leaving the feet.

Shinsplints: Aching in the front of the lower leg caused by pounding one's weight down onto a hard surface before conditioning has prepared the muscles for such exertion; the result is that muscles are tearing away from the bone.

Show: To move into or toward an offensive player's path to show him he is still being guarded, but without leaving the player who was first being defensed.

Shuffle: An offense in which players rotate from one spot to another until original positions are resumed.

Slowdown: Similar to a delay game in that the pace of the game is drastically slowed to throw off the tempo of a running team.

Spears reverse dribble: Bringing the ball back toward oneself prior to switching hands on the dribble, thus protecting it before taking it across the body in front of the defender.

Special play: A play designed specifically for a certain game situation or for use in a certain game or against a specific opponent.

Split the post: Two players crisscross around a post player and into the lane.

Squaring up: Bringing the shoulders in line with the target on a pass or shot.

Stall: Maintaining possession of the ball with passing and/or dribbling and without trying to score, usually to run out the clock when a team has a lead and sometimes to keep the score close (usually a team that is facing a superior team and wants to keep the ball as much as possible will use a delay game in which it attempts to score only after a certain length of possession or near the end of the quarter, but some teams have stalled for three quarters and tried to score only in the fourth).

Strong hand: The hand most used, usually the right.

Strong side: The side the ball starts on, and usually the side a majority of the players are on.

Stuff: Dunk; also to block someone's shot.

Superman drill: Making lay-ups on alternate sides without allowing the ball to touch the floor (this method is more correctly one of the Mikan drills), or rebounding the ball by throwing it against the board on opposite sides of the basket and jumping back and forth to rebound.

Take the charge: To allow an offensive player to collide with you in hopes of getting a foul called on him.

Tandem: Set up one behind the other and close together.

Ten-second line: The midcourt line when used to enforce a 10-second time limit for ball advancement.

Three seconds: The time allowed in the lane when on offense once you have stopped or changed directions (the count starts over when a shot goes up).

Timeline: The 10-second or midcourt line.

Tip: To push the ball toward a teammate or the basket without grabbing it first.

Top of the key: The point area.

Trap: To double-team a ball handler, usually along a sideline, so he cannot dribble free.

Triangle and two: A combination defense in which three players are zoning and two go man to man.

Turnover: Losing possession of the basketball due to a violation of rules or to mishandling the ball on the dribble or in passing.

Undercutting: A dangerous and, when intentional, unsportsman-like practice consisting of running under another player when he is already in the air attempting a shot.

Weak hand: The off hand.

Weak side: The side of the lane away from where the ball was when a play or pattern was initiated; usually a minority of the offensive players are stationed on this side.

Wing: The area beyond the free throw line and to the midcourt side of the baseline area.

Zone, zone defense: Guarding players who enter certain areas; most zones allow "slides" into areas where the ball or cutters go.

Zone offense: A pattern employed to score against a zone defense.

Zone press: A press in which players are stationed in key areas and attempt to intercept passes, trap, and put pressure on the primary pass receivers with movement out of those initial stations.

index